Animals in Danger

Animals in Danger

The 1974 Childcraft Annual

An Annual Supplement to
Childcraft—The How and Why Library

Field Enterprises Educational Corporation
Chicago Frankfurt London Paris Rome Sydney Tokyo Toronto

Acknowledgments

The publishers of *Childcraft—The How and Why Library*
gratefully acknowledge the courtesy of the following
publisher for permission to use a copyrighted illustration
appearing in this volume. Full illustration acknowledgments
appear on page 298.

Pages 206–207: Carl Iwasaki, Time/Life Books © 1963

Preface

They squawked and squabbled and waddled about on rocky beaches. They swam in the cold waters of the ocean. Thousands of them lived on islands and along the coasts of the North Atlantic Ocean. They were big, four-foot-tall birds, somewhat like penguins. They were called great auks.

You have never seen a great auk and you never will. There are no longer any great auks on the islands and coasts where they once lived. There are none in zoos. There are no photographs of any. The great auks are as gone as if they had never been. They were all killed by sailors who came to their islands and beaches and hunted them for food. None are left.

Could such a thing happen to any of the animals that are living now? Could it happen to the animals that you see in zoos, such as gorillas, tigers, and rhinoceroses? Could they someday be gone? Could they become animals you can only read about, like the great auk, and can never see?

Yes, that could happen!

At this very moment, more than a thousand different kinds of animals, in all parts of the world, are in very real danger. Scientists fear that many of them may soon be gone, just as the great auks are gone.

What animals are in danger? Why are they threatened? Is there any hope for them? Can they be saved? Is anyone doing anything to help them?

You'll find the answers to those questions in this book—*Animals in Danger*.

Animals in Danger

Contents

Vanished Animals of Long Ago

Never in the realm of nature have so many been exterminated by so few in so short a time.

Kai Curry-Lindahl

The last one

Makomo was on his way to the water hole to fill some pots when he saw the animal. He quickly hid behind some bushes to watch it.

The animal's hoofs made a *klop-klop-klop* sound on the hard, sun-baked ground. It trotted slowly toward the water hole, moving its head from side to side. It seemed to be sniffing the air. Perhaps it wanted to be sure that no hungry lion lay hidden nearby. When it came to the edge of the water hole, it lowered its head and began to drink.

Makomo was puzzled. He had never seen an animal like this one. It looked like a zebra, but its body was brown and its stripes were white. These stripes covered only its head and shoulders. What kind of animal could it be?

That night, Makomo told his father, Kama, about the strange new animal he had seen. What was it, he wondered. Where had it come from?

"I do not think it is a new animal from far away," said his father. "I think it is a quagga. When I was a little boy, as you are now, there were great herds of them in this land. But they have been gone for a long time. I did not think any were left."

"What happened to them?" asked Makomo.

"They were all killed," Kama replied. "The farmers shot them to feed their workers. They made bags of their skin, to put grain in. This quagga you have seen may be the last one."

Makomo thought about that. What would it be like to be the last one? How would he feel if he were the last person in the whole land? He would be lonely, he was sure. Was the quagga lonely?

Two days later, he saw the quagga at the water hole again. After that, he came every day to watch it. He squatted behind the bushes so that it would not see him and be frightened.

He came to know the quagga so well he could close his eyes and see it in his mind. Its coat was rich and shiny. Its eyes were brown, wise, and gentle. Its muzzle looked soft and velvety. He decided that it was the most beautiful of all animals.

He named it Beauty, and he talked to it in soft whispers. "One day I will let you see me, Beauty. But you will not be frightened. You will know that I mean you no harm. We will be friends. Then you will not be lonely any more."

And one day Beauty did see him. It had finished its drink and stood, head lifted, staring out over the plain into the setting sun. Abruptly, it snorted, turned its head, and looked straight at Makomo. It watched him for a long time. Then it snorted again. Tossing its head, the quagga raced off. Its hoofs drummed a song of wild freedom as it galloped away.

With shining eyes, Makomo watched it go. "When we are friends, Beauty," he whispered, "you will let me ride on you." He could not imagine anything more wonderful than to go flying across the plain on that brown, silky back.

Next day, Makomo did not hide. He sat in front of the bushes, without moving. The quagga came in sight, trotting steadily until it saw him. It stopped dead, watching him. He did not move. After a long time, the animal went to the water. It drank, pausing often to turn its head to look at him.

Each day, Makomo moved just a bit closer to the water hole. Always, he sat without moving a muscle, just watching while Beauty drank. At first the quagga was nervous, but after many days Makomo felt that it was getting to know him. It no longer paused when it saw him sitting near the water hole. The way it whisked its tail, tossed its head, and snorted was almost like a greeting. We are becoming friends, Makomo thought.

Then, one day, the quagga did not appear at the water hole. Makomo waited for it until the sun had set.

He went back the next day. Still there was no sign of Beauty. Worried, Makomo went to his father.

Kama looked at him sadly, and placed a hand on his head. "He was an animal, my son, and every animal walks near death. It may be that a farmer shot him. Perhaps one of our own people speared him. Or, he may have been killed by a lion. It is even possible that he has gone back to where he came from. But I fear that he is dead. It happens, Makomo. Death is a part of life. This is something you must understand."

There was a hard, hurting lump in Makomo's throat. He knew that his father was right. He would never see Beauty again. He could never become its friend.

But there was something that made him feel even worse. If Beauty had been a zebra, or a gemsbok, or an eland, he would have felt sad, too. But there was a difference. There were many zebras and gemsboks and elands. Beauty had been the *only* quagga—the last one. Now there were none.

There are many kinds of animals, but none like a quagga. Beauty had been a special creature, just as each kind of animal is rare, and special, and unlike any other. The earth would never again feel the beat of a quagga's galloping hoofs. The sun would never again shine on a quagga's brown, silky coat. Makomo knew that he was not the only one who had lost something wonderful. So had the whole world.

Why are they gone?

Millions of years ago, dinosaurs filled the world. They wallowed in great, green swamps and prowled through hot, damp forests in search of food. Some of them were the biggest animals that ever lived on land. Others were no larger than a chicken. There were dinosaurs with horns, dinosaurs with armored bodies, dinosaurs with bony bumps on their heads, and dinosaurs with bills like ducks. For more than a hundred million years these reptiles owned the earth.

Then, something happened. All the dinosaurs died out. This didn't happen quickly. It probably took hundreds or even thousands of years. But, as time passed, there were fewer and fewer dinosaurs. Finally, none were left. They had become extinct—a word that means that a whole family of living things has died out and is gone forever.

We don't know why the dinosaurs became extinct. We don't know why many other kinds of animals that lived long ago—flying reptiles, saber-toothed cats, and mammoths—became extinct. We can be sure, though, that people had nothing to do with it—because there were no people when most of these animals were living. But some kinds of animals have become extinct in just the past few hundred years. And we do know why this happened to them.

They were killed off by people.

fossil skeleton of the dinosaur Brontosaurus
at the Field Museum of Natural History, Chicago

Steller's sea cow

In the cold waters around islands off the coast of Siberia, there once lived a giant animal.

This animal was about twenty-five feet long and may have weighed as much as ten tons—bigger and heavier than an African elephant! It looked somewhat like a huge seal. In fact, it was a relative of the seal. The skin on its big body was black and thick and tough, like the bark of an old tree. This harmless creature lived in shallow water and spent most of its time eating seaweed. The sailors who first saw it named it "sea cow."

Sea cows were discovered in 1741. A few years later, fur hunters started coming to the islands to hunt seals and sea otters. They found that the meat of sea cows was good to eat, so they hunted these animals for food.

Even then, there were only about two thousand sea cows. They lived near the shore, in small herds. This made them easy to hunt. Less than thirty years after they were discovered, the hunters had killed them all. The giant, gentle sea cow was no more. It had joined a growing list of extinct animals.

The dodo

Have you ever read the book *Alice in Wonderland*? If you have, you've met the dodo. It's the fat, funny bird that Alice talks to after she climbs out of the pool of tears.

There really were birds called dodos, but they couldn't talk, of course. They lived on a little island in the Indian Ocean, not far from Africa. They were large, chubby birds, a little bigger than a big turkey. Their stubby wings were too small for flying and their legs were too short for running. So they sort of waddled wherever they went.

No people lived on the island. No one ever knew about it until the year 1507. Then, ships began to stop there for water and food. Sailors who went ashore to hunt had no trouble capturing the clumsy dodos. Dozens and dozens of the big birds were taken aboard ships and used for food.

People began living on the island in the 1600's. They, too, ate dodo birds. So did the dogs and pigs that people brought to the island. The dodos were easy to find and catch. They had no way of hiding or protecting themselves.

By 1681 there were no dodos left anywhere on the island. They had all been killed. The dodo was gone —forever.

model at the Field Museum of Natural History, showing what scientists think the dodo bird looked like

The blue buck

The blue buck was a beautiful animal, with glossy, bluish-brown fur. It lived in a small valley in South Africa.

People had lived there for hundreds of years. They hunted blue bucks and other animals. But with spears, and bows and arrows, they couldn't kill too many. Then, about three hundred years ago, people from Europe made South Africa their home. They had guns, and they rode horses, which made hunting easy.

South Africa was full of animals. The Europeans began to hunt many of them for their meat, for their skins, and for sport. Thousands of animals were killed each year. Many of these were blue bucks.

There weren't as many blue bucks as there were other kinds of animals, but the hunters did not care. They went on killing them. Each year there were fewer and fewer blue bucks. Still the killing went on. In the year 1800, the last one was shot. The blue buck was extinct.

The elephant bird

In one of the stories in the *Arabian Nights*, Sinbad the Sailor tells of a giant bird called a roc. The roc was so strong and so huge it could pick up an elephant in its claws!

There was never really a bird that big, of course. But many people believe that the story of the roc got started when people heard about a real giant bird that lived on an island near Africa. Of course, this bird wasn't as gigantic as the storybook roc. But it was about ten feet tall, which is pretty big for a bird. And it laid the biggest eggs in the world—they were bigger than basketballs!

Because of its size, this great bird is called the elephant bird. It looked somewhat like a huge, heavy ostrich. But it was probably a slow and clumsy runner. It had very small wings and was much too big and bulky to fly.

There were no big, meat-eating animals on the island to hunt the elephant birds, so the birds were safe. Then, people from Asia and Africa came to the island to live. They found that the meat of the elephant bird was good to eat, and began to hunt the birds. The birds were easy to hunt, for they could not fly and were too big to hide.

The last elephant birds were probably killed off more than three hundred years ago. This marvelous creature, one of the biggest birds that has ever lived, will never be seen again.

model at the Field Museum of Natural
History, Chicago, showing what scientists
think the elephant bird looked like

More and more

Since the year 1600, more than two hundred kinds of animals have become extinct!

Each jar on these pages represents one century—one hundred years—since 1600. In each jar there is one animal cooky for each kind of animal that became extinct during the century the jar stands for. You can see that in each new century, more animals became extinct than in the century before.

1600's   1700's

In the first jar there are seventeen cookies. Seventeen kinds of animals became extinct during the century from 1600 to 1699.

In the second jar there are thirty-six cookies. More than twice as many animals became extinct during the century from 1700 to 1799 as in the century before.

In the jar for 1800 to 1899, there are eighty-one cookies—nearly five times as many as in the first jar!

In the last jar there are eighty-three cookies. This jar stands for only seventy-three years. How many more animals will become extinct before this century ends?

1800's   **1900's**

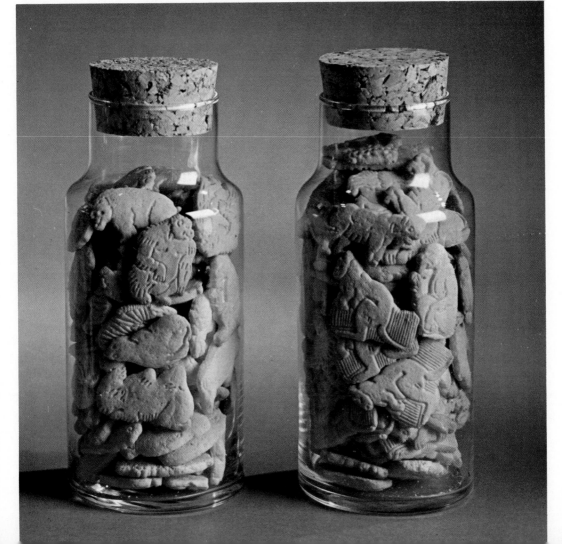

Keeping track

Everywhere in the world there are people who study animals. Scientists, naturalists, and other interested people often spend years watching certain kinds of animals. They keep careful records of the things they see and learn—and one of the things they keep track of is how many animals there are.

Scientists from several countries are working together to learn more about polar bears. These scientists have just put a bear to sleep with a special kind of gun.

Scientists paint numbers on the sleeping bears and put radio collars on them. The numbers identify the bears and show how many bears there are. The collars send out radio signals that help scientists keep track of the bears.

These people know that many kinds of animals are vanishing. Where they once saw thousands of animals, now there are only hundreds—sometimes only dozens. It is clear that these animals are in danger.

The smart, lively chimpanzee—the white-furred polar bear—the perky prairie dog—the clever giant otter—the proud, prowling tiger—all these and many, many other creatures may soon be gone forever. Like the quagga, the sea cow, the dodo, the blue buck, and the elephant bird, they will become extinct—unless we do something now.

Vanishing Animals Today

The blame will lie with us if the world becomes empty of many of the lovable creatures who not only have the same right to live as ourselves, but who are of vital importance to the balance of nature.

Joy Adamson

The empty woods

The late afternoon sun hung low and red in the sky. It sent long shadows slanting through the woods. The leaves of the trees were just changing into their fall colors. Where the sunlight touched them, they glowed red, purple, and gold.

A narrow, dirt path wound in and out among the trees, and three people were walking along it. One was a tall, pleasant-faced woman with gray hair. The other two were a boy and girl.

From time to time a soft breeze blew through the woods. Then the leaves of the trees would shiver with a rustling whisper. Except for this sound, and the buzz of insects, the forest was silent and peaceful. But from nearby there came the roar of cars and trucks on a big highway.

The woman and children rounded a turn in the path and came to a great, twisted, old oak tree. Down at the bottom of its gray trunk, where the tree's knobby

roots clutched the earth, there was an opening. It looked like the entrance to a tiny cave. Seeing this, the little girl scampered to the tree. She knelt down to peer into the hollow trunk. Moments later, she looked up at the woman, disappointment on her face.

"I thought maybe a little animal lived here, Grandma," she announced. "But there's just some wet leaves and a rusty old can."

The woman smiled, a bit sadly. "I'm afraid there aren't very many animals left in these woods, Susie," she said. "A few birds and squirrels are about all. There were lots of different kinds of animals here when I was a little girl, though."

"What kinds of animals?" questioned the boy.

"Well, there were deer, Georgie," replied his grandmother. "A small herd of deer. They were very shy, but I'd see them once in a while. And I would often see their hoof marks in the dirt."

"Where are they now?" George asked.

The woman gave a sad shake of her head. "I guess they went somewhere else. The forest is just too small for them now. It used to be much bigger, but most of it was cleared away and houses were built on the land."

"What other animals were there?" Susie wanted to know.

"Lots of frogs," her grandmother told her. "I haven't seen a frog here for years now, but there used to be thousands of them. Especially the tiny ones called spring peepers. In the evenings, in springtime, the woods were filled with the sound they made—like soft little bells ringing. Ching-ching-ching-ching."

"I know what a frog's like," Susie announced, bouncing on her toes with excitement. "There's a picture in my book. They're fat and green and bumpy, and they have great big mouths!"

Grandmother smiled. "I think that must be a picture of a bullfrog," she said. "They are bigger and fatter than the spring peepers. Bullfrogs make a sound like this"—she lowered her voice as much as she could—"CHUGGERUM!" The children laughed.

They had come to a tiny, slow-moving stream, crossed by a little stone bridge. Grandmother paused, looking down at the muddy bank and the still, brownish-colored water. Under the bridge, a broad patch of whitish scum floated on the surface of the water.

"Here is where most of the frogs used to live," said Grandmother. "I guess the water is too dirty for them now."

She pointed at a part of the bank not far from where they stood. "Right there, Susie, when I was just about your age, I found a big mud turtle lying on its back. The poor thing was waving its legs, trying to roll over. I turned him over and he crawled into the water and swam away. There were lots of turtles, but I'm afraid most of them were killed by cars after the big highway was built. They would wander out onto the road and get run over."

She sighed. "Thinking about it makes me sad. I miss them—the deer and the frogs and the turtles and all the other little creatures that are gone now."

"I miss 'em, too," the little girl declared.

George looked at her, scornfully. "How can you miss 'em? You never even saw 'em."

"I don't care!" she answered. "I *do* miss them! I wish they were still here so I could see them. It isn't fair!"

George looked at her for a moment. Then he looked down at the bank. He tried to imagine a fat mud turtle lying on its back, waving its legs. He saw himself scrambling down the bank to help it. He tried to imagine the footprints of the deer. He tried to hear the soft *ching-ching-ching* of the spring peepers.

But he couldn't. Those things were gone. He would never have them. Suddenly, he felt cheated.

"You're right!" he said, scowling. "It isn't fair!"

Africa

The chimpanzee

The first, faint light of dawn crept into the sky, pushing out night's darkness. One by one the stars faded. Morning had come to the African rain forest.

High in a tree, a chimpanzee woke up. He had spent the night sleeping in a nest made of bent and twisted branches. He lazily yawned and scratched himself for several minutes. Then he climbed down from the tree and started out to find his morning meal.

The chimpanzee walked on all fours, his body bent forward, the knuckles of his hands touching the ground. If he had walked upright, like a man, he would have stood nearly five feet tall.

In a few minutes, the chimpanzee found a tree that seemed to promise breakfast. He hurried into its branches. Sure enough, there were plenty of tasty leaf buds for a hungry chimp.

He munched contentedly. Suddenly, from a nearby part of the forest came a loud uproar—barking, chattering, screaming, and hooting! The chimpanzee stared in the direction of the sound. The hair on his body stood up with excitement. He leaped down from the tree and hurried toward the noise.

The clamor came from a clump of fig trees. There, more than a dozen chimpanzees scrambled about in the branches. The trees were full of ripe, juicy fruit, and the chimps were wild with excitement. Here was a feast!

The chimpanzee on the ground greeted the ones in the trees with hooting noises. He knew them all,

because he traveled through the forest with them. They
hooted greetings back at him.

He leaped into the tree. Before hurrying to find a
good feeding place, he stopped, put his hand on the
back of another male chimpanzee, and gave him a few
scratches. He was showing his respect for the leader
of the group.

For most of the morning the band of chimpanzees
stayed in the fig trees, eating their fill. As they
ate, they gave little grunts of pleasure.

As the sun rose high in the sky, the forest grew hot.
Except for the steady whirr of insects there was
silence. The chimpanzees dozed in the shade of leafy
branches, or sat scratching in each other's fur.
Young chimps, two or three years old, chased wildly

back and forth through the vines and branches.
Sometimes, a grown-up would reach out and tickle
one of the little ones.

By late afternoon the forest was cool. The
chimpanzees trooped off in search of a new feeding
place. As the sun set, the forest filled with shadows.
The chimps began to make sleeping nests in the nearest
trees. Each animal, except for the very young ones,
made its own nest and slept by itself. Mothers and
babies curled up together in the mother's nest.

Night came to the forest. The moon painted the tops

of the trees with silver. In their leafy tree beds, the chimpanzees slept, untroubled by anything.

But the chimpanzees of Africa are in trouble, even though they do not know it. In some parts of Africa, these clever and amusing creatures—so much like humans in so many ways—are being hunted by humans for food. In other places, the forests where they live are being cut down to make room for houses and farms. Some scientists fear that in just a few more years these wonderful creatures may be gone from the wild—forever.

The indri

The indri is somewhat like a monkey with a dog's face. It lives high in the treetops in a small part of a hot, wet, mountainside forest.

Soon after sunrise each day, the forest fills with loud howling that means the indri is awake. During the morning, little groups of three, four, or five of these creatures move about together in the trees, feeding on leaves. Sometimes they sit on branches and sunbathe, stretching their arms above their heads as if they are worshiping the sun. In the hot afternoon hours they sleep. But in the evening, they are noisy and active again.

When an indri comes down from the trees and walks on the ground, it looks like a little furry man. It hops along on its legs, with its body swaying and its arms spread out for balance, like a tightrope walker. When it stands upright this way, it is about three feet tall.

The indri is timid and peaceful. It eats leaves, fruits, nuts, buds, and flowers, and it tries to hide from people. But it is in bad trouble. Its forest home is slowly being cut down—huge areas are gone already. The indri has nowhere else to go, for it can find food only in the place where it now lives.

The crocodile

The dinosaurs all died out about 70 million years ago. But in Africa there is an animal that is very much like a dinosaur! It is a big, fierce, scaly, meat-eating reptile—the crocodile.

Most African crocodiles live near slow-moving rivers and streams. They like to lie on the riverbanks in the hot sun, and swim in the cool, brown waters. Mother crocodiles dig shallow pits in the sandy banks in which to lay their eggs. The mother covers the eggs with sand and guards them. When the babies hatch, they make little croaking noises. Then the mother digs away the sand and sets the babies free.

Small crocodiles eat fish. Big crocodiles, which can grow as long as sixteen feet, eat large animals. These big ones often lie in wait for antelope and other animals to come to the river to drink. When the animal puts its head down to the water, the crocodile grabs the animal's head or leg in its jaws. It pulls the animal into the water and twists it around and around, drowning it and tearing it apart! Crocodiles often attack young hippopotamuses, and have attacked people, too.

Crocodiles are the largest of all reptiles. Because they are so much like dinosaurs, scientists want to save them for study. But crocodiles are becoming extinct. In parts of Africa, many have been killed off because people think they are dangerous pests. Many others have been killed for their skins, which are used to make such things as shoes and purses.

The African wild dog

As dawn lights up the sky of South Africa, a wild dog pack gets ready for the morning hunt. The dogs touch their noses together. They jump playfully at each other, wagging their tails. Then, off they go. One dog stays behind to guard the pups that are hidden in the den.

There are usually from ten to twenty dogs in a pack. They hunt by spreading out in a long line. Silently, they trot across the vast yellow plain.

The dogs move toward a herd of wildebeests. When the wildebeests see the dogs, they take to their heels. The dogs streak after them, yipping with excitement. The hunt is on!

One wildebeest soon becomes tired and slows down. The dogs quickly close in on it. Some of them cut in

front of it, separating it from the rest of the herd.
Surrounded and exhausted, the wildebeest stops. The
dogs swarm over it and pull it down.

They are soon feasting on the wildebeest's flesh.
As they eat, they never snarl or snap at each other
as tame dogs often do. The wild dogs of Africa get
along very well with each other. They share almost
everything.

When the dogs have eaten all they can hold, they
hurry back to the den. There they spit out chunks
of meat for the guard dog and the puppies.

The wild dogs do an important job. They help keep
things in balance by holding down the numbers of
many kinds of animals. But the wild dogs are in
danger. Many people dislike them. They have been
hunted and poisoned until not many are left.

The mountain gorilla

You probably shiver at the thought of meeting a big, shaggy, fierce-looking wild gorilla. A full-grown mountain gorilla may stand six feet tall and weigh as much as three men. It could easily crush you.

But gorillas are really very gentle and peaceful. Several scientists, both men and women, have lived close to groups of wild gorillas—and made friends with them!

These big, shaggy creatures live in forests. They travel about in groups in search of food. They eat leaves, bark, fruits, flowers, and the tender shoots of plants. They seldom eat meat, or drink water—they get all the water they need from the juicy plants they eat.

Gorillas spend their days eating and sleeping. While grown-ups take naps, the young gorillas play and wrestle and chase one another, just as children do. At night, each grown-up makes itself a nest of vines and branches to sleep in. Mothers and babies sleep together.

Gorillas are four-footed animals. They walk on their feet and the knuckles of their hands. Although they sometimes climb trees, they never swing through the trees, as some people believe. They are mainly ground animals.

There are two kinds of gorillas: lowland gorillas and mountain gorillas. Both kinds are in trouble, but the mountain gorillas face the greatest danger. People are slowly taking over their lands. As the gorillas have less land in which to move around, there is less food for them. If too much of their land is taken, they may not be able to survive.

The African lammergeyer

On great wings that have a spread of nearly nine feet, a lammergeyer soars over its mountain home. Its sharp eyes peer down, searching for food. It eats the meat, skin, and bones of dead animals.

When the lammergeyer sees an animal lying on the ground, it flies slowly around and around and around. It watches and waits to make sure the animal is dead. Sometimes a lammergeyer finds only a pile of bones, but this is food, too. The great bird flies into the air with a bone in its beak. When it is high up, it lets the bone fall and smash on the rocks below. Then the lammergeyer glides down and eats the marrow out of the smashed bone.

These birds, also called "bearded vultures," help to keep the world clean by getting rid of the bodies of dead animals. They do not cause people any trouble. But they are slowly being wiped out—by accident.

Lammergeyers live in pairs, high in the mountains. Here they build very large nests of sticks, fur, and bones. From their mountaintop nests, the lammergeyers fly out over the surrounding countryside in search of food. Too often they find death instead. People sometimes put out chunks of poisoned meat to kill jackals that eat sheep. The lammergeyers eat the poisoned meat and die. And so, each year, there are fewer and fewer lammergeyers.

The white rhinoceros

A bright full moon hangs in the blue-black sky. It floods the land with cool light, turning the broad African plain into a great silvery sea of grass. Here and there on the plain, shadowy clusters of trees and bushes look like dark, shaggy islands.

A huge, bulky gray beast is feeding on the grass. The moonlight gleams on the two horns that stick up from its long nose. It is a male white rhinoceros. The biggest of all rhinos, it is more than six feet high at the shoulders and about fifteen feet long. This great animal weighs almost four tons.

All night long the big animal eats, for it takes a lot of grass to fill that great body. As he stands chewing the tough grass in his big, square mouth, his tubelike ears never stop moving. They twitch and twist and turn in every direction, listening for the slightest sound. The rhino cannot see very well. He depends more on his keen senses of hearing and smell to tell him what is happening around him.

By midmorning the plain begins to grow hot under the fierce African sun. The rhino is comfortably full. Big feet thudding on the earth, he trots off across the plain. He looks quite clumsy. But in spite of his size and weight, he can run as fast as a race horse for a short distance.

The rhino hurries across the plain until he comes to a large, shallow pool of rain water. This is his mud wallow. He ambles to the pool's edge, dips his nose into the water, and drinks for a long time. Then he flops down to wallow in the mud. He rolls over, first on one side, then on the other side. After smearing

(continued on page 56)

The white rhinoceros

(continued from page 55)

himself thickly with mud, he rests his chin on the
ground and goes to sleep.

Under the hot sun, the mud dries into a hard crust.
This crust protects the rhino's body from the many
kinds of biting flies and insects that can make even his
tough skin smart and itch.

For millions of years rhinos have lived this kind of
life—eating, sleeping, and wallowing in their muddy
pools or in piles of dust. Once, there were rhinos in
most parts of the world, even in Europe and North
America. Today, there are only a few rhinos—and only
in parts of Africa and Asia. All the rhinos are in danger,
but the white rhinos of Africa are in the most danger.
For many years they have been hunted for their
horns, which some people believe have magic powers.
Today, there are only about 250 white rhinos left.

The aye-aye

On a large island off the coast of Africa lives a strange little animal called the aye-aye.

The aye-aye is about the size of a cat. It lives in trees and comes out only at night. Then it leaps about among the tree branches in search of food. Most of the time the aye-aye is silent, but sometimes it makes a noise that sounds like "aye-aye." That's how it got its name.

The aye-aye has strange-looking hands. The middle finger on each hand is much longer and thinner than the other fingers. The aye-aye eats and drinks with these two long fingers. To get food, the aye-aye chews tiny holes in tree trunks, then it reaches in and pulls out little caterpillars that it eats. And to drink, it dips one long finger into water and then pulls the finger sideways through its mouth!

The aye-aye is one of the most endangered of all animals. The forests where it lives have nearly all been cut down. Many people try to kill aye-ayes when they see them, because they believe that aye-ayes bring bad luck. So the aye-aye is in bad trouble. Only about fifty of these odd little animals remain in the whole world.

The walia ibex

In the rugged mountains of Ethiopia, high among towering cliffs and crags, lives the walia ibex. This animal belongs to the goat family. Like all mountain goats, it is wonderfully sure-footed and perfectly at home as it trots along narrow ledges thousands of feet high.

The male walia ibex is about three feet tall at the shoulders. It has enormous curved horns that are more than forty inches long. Its fur is dark brown on the back and shoulders, and whitish on the stomach and insides of the legs. The female ibex is smaller and lighter colored, and has small horns.

The females and their young usually live in small herds of five to twenty animals, led by an old female. The males live by themselves much of the time, but in the fall they join a herd for a while. In spring and summer, the ibexes stay near the very tops of the mountains. In winter, when snow piles up thickly on the mountaintops and icy winds roar, the ibexes move down into mountain meadows. They eat grass and leafy plants.

On its high mountaintops, the walia ibex is safe from all enemies but one. That enemy is man. It is against Ethiopian law to shoot an ibex, but many people hunt them for their meat, skins, and horns. There are probably only a few hundred of these mountain goats left.

The Tana River mangabey

High in a tree, in a shadowy, gloomy forest, two tiny moons seem to be shining. These "moons" are the pale, nearly white, eyelids of a kind of monkey called the Tana River mangabey. Sitting in the shadows, the mangabey's body can hardly be seen. But its white eyelids shine like little lights.

The mangabey is resting now. Earlier, it was scurrying through the trees with other mangabeys, looking for leaves and fruit to eat. But it didn't eat everything it found. Instead, it stuffed some of the leaves into the large pouches in its cheeks. Now it is enjoying a snack of those stored-up leaves.

Like most monkeys, mangabeys are expert climbers and jumpers. Most monkeys are also noisy. They chatter or scream or howl almost constantly. But not mangabeys. Mangabeys are usually very quiet and shy. Because they are gentle, they sometimes make friendly pets.

Mangabeys once lived throughout a large forest along the Tana River, in Kenya, Africa. But now they have been pushed into a small area. Much of the forest where they used to live has been cut down and turned into farmland. More forest will probably be cut down in the future. The Tana River mangabeys are in grave danger.

The addax

The home of the addax is the barren, sandy wastes of the Sahara. Here, small herds, led by an old male, travel about searching for tough desert grass to eat. An addax can live in parts of the desert where not even a camel can stay alive. In fact, an addax can go for weeks, and even months, without taking a

drink of water! It gets all the water it needs from the plants it eats.

The addax is a member of the antelope family. It is an animal that changes its color. In winter, its coat is grayish-brown, but its summer coat is milky white. An addax is about three feet high. Its graceful, curling horns are often more than a yard long. Its short tail, which looks like a piece of rope, seems to wiggle all the time.

Even though the addax lives in the deepest parts of the desert, it isn't safe. It is not a fast runner. A man on a horse or a camel can catch it easily. The desert Arabs have hunted it until not many are left. Only a few thousand addax still live in the Sahara—and they are still being hunted.

Asia

The Bengal tiger

Golden eyes gleaming, the great Bengal tiger prowled through the tall grass of the meadow. It was near sundown, and the grass glowed deep orange in the light of the red, setting sun. With his orange-red body and black stripes, the tiger could hardly be seen as he moved through the orange, shadow-filled grass.

Slowly, the sun dropped out of sight. Blackness filled the sky. This was the tiger's hunting time. He had not eaten for several days and was ready for a hearty meal.

Hours passed, and the tiger prowled on. Once, he met another tiger. The two big cats rubbed their heads together in greeting. Then each went on its way into the night in search of food.

Suddenly, the tiger stopped. He could see well in the darkness, and about a hundred yards ahead of him stood a young water buffalo, calmly grazing.

The tiger pressed his body close to the ground and began to move again. He looked almost like a big, striped snake sliding through the tall grass.

The distance between the tiger and his prey became less and less. The buffalo continued to munch mouthfuls of grass, unaware of any danger. Now the two animals were only thirty feet apart.

The tiger stood up. He lifted his tail. Then, with a terrifying roar, he charged! His nine-foot-long, four-hundred-pound body moved in one enormous leap and came smashing down on the startled buffalo's back. As the buffalo fell to the ground, the tiger buried his teeth in its throat.

All night long the tiger ate, gobbling nearly fifty

pounds of meat! When the sun came up, the tiger
dragged the buffalo's body to a hiding place among
some rocks. Then the big striped cat settled down to
bask in the warm morning sun. After a while, he
yawned a great yawn that showed all his sharp teeth.
Flopping over onto his back, he went to sleep. After
his enormous meal, and with plenty of "leftovers," the
tiger would not have to hunt again for several days.

Only fifty years ago there were about forty
thousand tigers living in India. But for many years,
people hunted tigers for their heads and skins.
Thousands of tigers were killed by hunters.

Today, there are probably less than two thousand.

It is now against the law to hunt tigers in India. But many lawbreakers do hunt them. They sell the skins to people who make coats of them. Many tigers are also shot and poisoned by farmers, because the tigers kill farm animals for food. But the tigers are forced to do this because their hunting areas are being turned into farms and villages. There are fewer animals for tigers to hunt, and fewer places in which they can hunt.

Tigers are in trouble, not only in India but in other parts of Asia. And wild tigers are found only in Asia. Perhaps someday soon, the only tigers left in the world will be those living in zoos.

The orang-utan

Orang-utans seem to be the world's sleepiest animals! They go to bed before it's dark. They get up late in the morning. And they spend most of the day taking naps!

These long-armed, red-furred apes live in warm, wet forests on the islands of Borneo and Sumatra. Long ago, the people who lived on the islands believed that the apes were just a different kind of men who wanted to live in the woods. That's why the people named them *orang-utan*, which means "man of the woods."

Orang-utans aren't as big as their cousins, the gorillas and chimpanzees. A full-grown male orang is usually only about four feet tall. And orang-utans don't spend most of the time on the ground as chimps and gorillas do—they live in the trees. Orang-utans move about in search of leaves, fruit, buds, insects, birds' eggs, and bark to eat. At night, they make nests of branches to sleep in. They often build a little "roof" over a nest to keep rain out.

Orang-utans have only one enemy—people. Lumber companies are rapidly cutting down the forests where the orangs live. And people hunt the orangs. The hunters kill mother orangs and take the babies to sell as pets or to zoos. But most of the babies die because the hunters do not know how to take care of them.

There are probably less than five thousand orang-utans left. How long will it be before they are all gone?

The gaur

It was sunset, and the little herd of gaurs began to move toward the forest clearing where they spent their nights. They moved slowly, munching on grass as they went.

Suddenly, one of the gaurs gave a whistling snort. She stretched her head toward a nearby clump of bushes and made a sound like a low, growling moo. This told the other gaurs that there was an enemy in the bushes! Quickly, they all bunched together.

There was a tiger in the bushes. Two of the male gaurs raised their heads and pulled back their lips to show their teeth. They grunted and stamped their front feet, as if to say, "Attack if you dare!"

But the tiger didn't care to attack such big, powerful, horned beasts. It slunk away into the forest.

Gaurs are wild oxen—cousins of cows and bulls. But gaurs are the biggest oxen in the world. The head of a six-foot-tall man would barely reach to the shoulder of a full-grown bull gaur.

Farmers often drive herds of tame cattle onto the gaurs' grazing places—and the gaurs catch a sickness from the cattle. Many of them have died from this sickness. And the forests where they live are being cut down, as well. So, with each year, there are fewer and fewer of these big wild oxen.

The snow leopard

Most people think of leopards as being large, black-spotted, orange cats. But a snow leopard has smoky-gray fur with black spots shaped like rings. And most people think of leopards as living in hot forests. But snow leopards live high in the cold, rocky mountains of central Asia, where patches of white snow lie among the brown boulders.

A snow leopard isn't as big as a lion or a tiger, but it's still a very big cat. A full-grown snow leopard is often more than six feet long and may weigh as much as a hundred pounds.

A snow leopard likes to live by itself. Each snow

leopard has its own den. Usually this is just a shallow cave where the leopard sleeps. The leopards hunt by themselves, too. They roam among the cliffs and crags, searching for wild goats and other animals that live in the mountains. They creep in close to a herd and leap onto one of the animals from a boulder. A snow leopard usually feeds for several days on an animal it has killed. It stays near the dead animal to guard it from vultures and crows.

Snow leopards are sometimes shot by farmers because the leopards attack the farmers' herds of tame sheep and goats. But the snow leopard is mostly in trouble just because it is beautiful—hunters can get a lot of money for its silky, smoky fur. So these beautiful animals are becoming very rare.

The dragon of Komodo

The dragon was hungry. For several hours it had been hiding beside a trail used by deer coming down from the mountain. The dragon waited, hidden beneath a fallen tree. Its forked tongue darted in and out, like a flickering flame.

Klip-klop-klippa-klop.

There was a sound of hoofs on the trail. Three deer appeared, moving along one after the other. All morning they had been feeding on grass high up on the hot, sunny mountainside. Now, they wanted to find a cool, shady place in the forest where they could sleep.

Klip-klop-klippa-klop.

Suddenly, the huge, scaly dragon lunged out at the first deer! Sharp, savage teeth sank into one of the deer's thin legs. The deer kicked and struggled in

(continued on page 80)

The dragon of Komodo

(continued from page 79)

panic, trying to free itself. Its companions raced away in terror.

The deer fell to the ground, its leg nearly cut in half by the dragon's teeth. Instantly, the dragon ripped open the deer's stomach, killing it. Then the big, scaly monster began to feed, gulping down huge chunks of deer—hide, hair, bones, and all!

The dragon is not a real dragon, of course. But it's the closest thing in the world to a real dragon. It is one of the giant lizards, called Komodo dragons, that live on the island of Komodo and several other small islands in Indonesia.

The Komodo dragon is the largest of all lizards, and one of the biggest of all reptiles. Komodo dragons may grow to be as much as ten feet long. They may weigh up to three hundred pounds. With their sharp teeth and claws, they are fierce hunters. A full-grown Komodo dragon can even attack and kill a big water buffalo!

The islands where the Komodo dragons live and hunt may soon be "opened up" by companies searching for minerals and oil. If this happens, the Komodo dragons will be in trouble. If too much of their hunting ground is lost to mines and oil wells, the dragons could be wiped out.

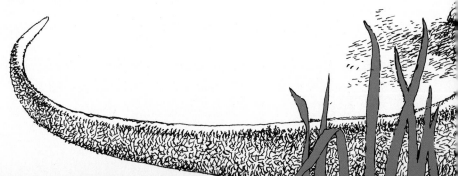

The swamp deer

The swamp deer of India is one of the most beautiful
of all deer. In summer, its coat is reddish-brown
and covered with pale spots. In winter, its coat turns
golden-brown. It lives in swampy grasslands.
With its broad, spreading hoofs, it can walk easily
on the wet, spongy ground. Grass, buds, leaves, and
small leafy plants are its main food. But best of all,
it likes the tall, juicy reeds that wave in the wind at
the edges of lakes and ponds.

In spring, summer, and fall, swamp deer live in
small herds. A herd may be made up of all males, all
females, or males and females together. In winter,
the deer gather together in large herds.

Each year the herds are getting smaller. Most of
the swamps where the deer used to live have been
drained and the land turned into farms. Slowly, the
deer have been pushed into other places where there is
hardly enough room for them. Even though swamp
deer are protected by law, many people hunt them for
their meat and antlers. There are only a few thousand
of these beautiful, wild swamp deer left.

The Indian rhinoceros

Long ago, according to an old legend told in India, the god Krishna wanted the rhinoceros to fight for him in a battle. He dressed the big beast in armor, but soon found that it was too stupid to obey orders. So Krishna sent it away. But he forgot to take back the armor. To this day, the rhinoceros still wears its "armor" of thick, bumpy skin.

Most Indian rhinoceroses are about six feet high and fourteen feet long. They look slow and clumsy, but they can gallop as fast as a horse for short distances. And, surprising as it may seem, they can even jump and swim and dive very well.

Indian rhinos live in forests and on grassy plains. They eat grass and leafy twigs. They like to live alone, but they often gather in small groups and wallow in water holes and ponds.

For many years, the Indian rhinoceros has been hunted for its horn, which some people believe is magical. These animals have also been driven out of the places where they live as land is taken for farms. Even though it is against the law, some people still hunt them. Their numbers are getting fewer and fewer. There are probably less than seven hundred Indian rhinos left in the wild.

The douc langur

The douc langur is also known as the "painted monkey." It's easy to see why, for it is one of the most brightly colored of all monkeys. It looks as if someone had painted its fur. In fact, it seems to be wearing a colorful costume—a dark brown cap, a gray jacket, a white vest, knee-length black pants, and reddish-brown stockings!

This monkey is a mystery. All we really know about it is what it looks like and how big it is—about thirty inches long, not counting its long tail. Very little is known about the way it lives. We don't even

know for sure what it eats. The douc langur stays
hidden deep in the forests of Southeast Asia. No one
has been able to find out much about it.

We do know, however, that the douc langur may be
in bad trouble. For many years, war has been raging
where the douc langur lives. Huge parts of its forest
home have been destroyed. Scientists are not sure
that this brightly colored creature can survive. It
can't be saved easily, as some animals can, by being
put into zoos. When douc langurs are put into cages,
they often simply die. It would be sad, indeed, if the
painted monkey became extinct just because it was
caught in the middle of a quarrel among people.

The Ceylon elephant

Do you know how to tell an Asian elephant from an African elephant? You can tell them apart by the size of their ears. An African elephant has big, floppy ears that look like fans. An Asian elephant's ears are much smaller.

The Ceylon elephant is an Asian elephant. It lives on the big island of Sri Lanka, which used to be known as Ceylon. Ceylon elephants live mainly in thick, green forests. They spend most of their time just eating—leaves, grass, vines, the tender shoots of plants, and fruit. They love to wallow in mud holes and bathe in streams.

A grown-up male Ceylon elephant is about nine feet tall. The older male elephants live by themselves. The females live in herds, with their little ones, and sometimes with a few young males. There are usually from ten to fifty elephants in a herd, and the leader is usually the oldest female in the herd.

Once there were many thousands of wild Ceylon elephants. Today, there are less than three thousand left. Most of the forests where they once roamed have been cut down. The few parts of forest that are left have been turned into national parks, but the parks are not really big enough for the elephants. These animals need lots of room in order to find food. So, in their search for food, the elephants sometimes leave the forests and cause damage to nearby farms. Many elephants have been shot by angry farmers. Unless the Ceylon elephants can be given more room and better protection, they may soon be gone from the wild.

North America

The timber wolf

It was early spring. For months, winter snow had covered the land like a white blanket. But the snow had melted until only small patches were left. Tiny new plants were pushing pale green heads out of the damp, brown earth.

Six baby wolves peeped out at the world from the entrance of a den dug among the roots of a tall pine tree. These short-legged, roly-poly balls of brown fur were only a few weeks old. But they would grow quickly. Soon they would be bold enough to go outside the den. They would play and explore. They would smell new smells and learn about being wolves. Their parents would teach them how to hunt.

In about a year, the cubs would leave their parents. In two years, they would have mates and families of their own. But their parents would stay together and have more cubs, for wolves usually stay with their mates for life.

Right now, the little cubs watched with bright eyes
the things that were happening outside the den.
In the twilight, their father and several other wolves
were getting ready to hunt. The big wolves wagged
their tails and playfully leaped at each other. After
a while, they lifted their pointed noses to the sky
and howled—long wails that floated off on the wind.

The howling went on for several minutes. Then
the pups' father and his companions trotted off. The
pups' mother, who had been howling with the others,
returned to the den. She lay down. At once, the pups

began to climb and scramble playfully over her. They nudged her with their noses, growled tiny play growls, and pretended to attack her tail.

Meanwhile, the hunters trotted through the darkness, looking for food. They were also doing the job that nature had given them—the job of helping to keep things in balance. When the wolves found a herd of elk, deer, or caribou, they would chase them. If there was a weak or sick animal in the herd, the wolves would go after it because it couldn't run as fast as the others. By killing sick, unhealthy

animals, wolves help the herds of elk, deer, and
caribou to stay strong and healthy. And the wolves
also keep the herds from becoming so large that they
eat up too many plants and spoil the land.

Actually, elk, deer, and caribou are not a wolf's only
food. Strange as it may seem, wolves also eat lots
of mice! During summertime, one wolf may catch and
eat as many as two dozen mice a day. In the places
where they live, wolves are a great help in keeping
mice from increasing too much. That's a very good
thing, because too many mice can spoil large areas of
land very quickly.

For hundreds of years, people all over the world
have believed that wolves are cruel, bloodthirsty
beasts. There are many fairy tales and folk tales in
which the wolf is the symbol of evil. There are also
old reports of wolves attacking people and eating
them. Today, scientists know that most of these
reports are not true. Many scientists and naturalists
have spent months living near wolves to study
them. They were often alone, with wolves all around
them. But they were never attacked or threatened.
They found that wolves are smart, brave, good-natured
animals that seem curious about people. Some people
have even raised wolf cubs as pets and found that
they are much like dogs.

But people have feared and hated wolves for a long
time. Wolves have been hunted, trapped, and poisoned
without mercy. Governments have even paid money
for every wolf that was killed.

At one time, timber wolves—also called gray
wolves—lived in almost every part of North America.
Today, there are about twenty thousand wolves left
in all of Canada, and probably less than a thousand in
the United States.

The pine-barrens tree frog

Kwank-kwank-kwank-kwank.

A pine-barrens tree frog sits on a twig. His throat swells up like a bubble as he makes his *kwank* sound. He is a male, and he is calling for a female to come to him and be his mate. It is springtime—mating time—and soon the female frogs will lay masses of eggs in the water. Out of the eggs will come tiny wriggling tadpoles that look much like baby fish.

Many of the tadpoles get eaten by fish and other water creatures. But before the end of summer, those left grow front and back legs. They lose their fishlike tails. Now they are grown-up frogs, about one and one-half inches long. Little suction cups on their toes help them climb trees and hang from the underside of large leaves. The little frogs jump and dart about after insects to eat.

At the first touch of cold weather, the frogs burrow down into the mud of ponds, or dig down under rocks or logs. There they stay all winter, stiff and unmoving, only half alive. They will remain this way until the spring sunshine warms them up.

Most of the places where the little pine-barrens tree frogs once lived have become towns, farms, and factories. Almost all of the frogs now live in a tiny swamp in the Pine Barrens pine tree forest in New Jersey.

Some people want to drain this swamp and turn it into an airport. If this happens, the frogs will have lost their last home, for they have no other place nearby where they can live. Then this colorful little tree frog will probably become extinct.

The black-tailed prairie dog

Prairie dogs aren't really dogs. They're chubby, chattering members of the squirrel family. They got their name because they live on prairies—broad grasslands, mountain meadows, and grassy deserts—and because they make a shrill barking sound, like a dog.

Prairie dogs live in "towns" made up of many underground burrows. The animals dig the burrows with their sharp little claws. Each burrow has a long tunnel that goes almost straight down for twelve feet or more. At the bottom there are "rooms" for sleeping and storing food. There is also a tunnel leading to a hidden "back door" for time of danger. At the front entrance is a mound of dirt that keeps water from running into the burrow. Prairie dogs often sit on these mounds to watch for enemies.

All day long, the fat little animals pop in and out of their burrows. They hunt for food, repair their "front porch" mounds, and frisk with each other. When two prairie dogs meet, they usually give each other a "kiss"! Their favorite food is grass—tender young grass sprouts, grass roots, and grass seeds. They also like dandelion stems and flowers. Sometimes they eat grasshoppers.

About one hundred years ago there were *billions* of prairie dogs living in many enormous "towns" in western North America. But for years these little animals have been treated as pests. People have killed them by the hundreds of thousands with poisoned food and poison gas. Now their numbers are much, much less. They have vanished from many of the places where they once lived.

The kit fox

Kit foxes are the smallest of all North American foxes. In fact, they got their name—kit—because they're not much bigger than a kitten. They have another name, too. They are sometimes called "swift foxes," because they run so fast.

Deserts and prairies are the kit foxes' home. During the day, the foxes sleep in their underground burrows. At night, they come out to hunt. Like their big cousins, wolves and dogs, kit foxes eat meat. They eat almost any small creature they can catch—rabbits, mice, kangaroo rats, lizards, and grasshoppers.

Kit fox families are much like wolf families. When a male and female fox becomes mates, they find a

burrow and start a family. When their babies are
born, both the mother and father care for them and
teach them things. The babies play together just like
puppies. When they grow up, they leave the den to
find their own mates and start their own families.
But the mother and father kit foxes stay together as
long as they live.

People have never tried to kill off all kit foxes on
purpose, as they have wolves and some other animals.
But many kit foxes have been killed, mostly by
accident. They often live in the same places as
coyotes. When people put out traps and poison for the
coyotes, kit foxes were often trapped and poisoned
instead. Many others have been killed by dogs.
Now there are not very many of these dainty little
foxes left.

The whooping crane

Ker-loo! Ker-lee-oo!

The loud cry of the whooping cranes rings through the air like a bugle call. It is spring, and the big birds are rising up into the sky to begin their long journey to the north.

In winter, the whooping cranes live in a tiny, marshy place on the coast of Texas. In spring, the whole whooping crane flock flies to a wild part of northern Canada. They spend the summer in a wet, marshy place like the one in Texas. There the cranes mate, build their nests, lay their eggs, and hatch their baby chicks. In autumn, the cranes fly south, back to Texas.

The whooping crane is a big, grand bird. It is the tallest bird in North America—often more than five feet tall. When a big whooping crane spreads its wings, they may measure seven feet from tip to tip. With its long legs, a whooping crane easily wades in shallow water to look for food. It eats frogs, crayfish, shellfish, snakes, many kinds of insects, and several kinds of plants.

Some 150 years ago there were many whooping cranes in the wild parts of North America. But more and more people moved into the places where the cranes lived. The big birds were hunted and shot by the hundreds. Their eggs were stolen from their nests. Finally, only a few whoopers were left.

Today, there are less than a hundred of these beautiful big birds. The United States and Canadian governments protect them. Whooping cranes are still in danger—but there is hope for them.

The grizzly bear

"Grizzled" means "gray-haired." Grizzly bears got this name because many of them have white-tipped fur that gives them a grayish or "grizzled" look. But there are also dark-brown, light-brown, tan, cream-colored, and nearly black grizzlies.

A large grizzly may be four and one-half feet high at the shoulders and weigh as much as eight hundred pounds. If it stands up on its back legs, it may be eight or nine feet tall. These big animals eat all sorts of things—nuts, acorns, honey, berries, insects, roots, mushrooms, grass, fish, frogs, snakes, elk, deer, beaver, and moose. Much of the meat they eat comes from large, dead animals they find, such as elk and moose. But the grizzlies also hunt elk, moose, and deer, and dig for ground squirrels and marmots.

In late autumn, before the harsh winter weather begins, a grizzly digs itself a big, roomy den. It makes a bed of leaves, grass, and twigs. Then it goes to sleep. But bears don't sleep, or hibernate, all winter. They sometimes wake up and leave their dens to get fresh air and exercise. Mothers and their young cubs sleep in the same den. Sometimes, young half-grown bears share the same den.

Hundreds of thousands of grizzly bears once roamed throughout North America. But for many years, grizzlies were shot and poisoned by the thousands because people feared them. They were also a problem because they sometimes killed cows and sheep. Now they are found only in a few national parks and some wild parts of Alaska, Canada, and perhaps Mexico. The grizzly bear is becoming extinct.

(continued on page 106)

The grizzly bear
(continued from page 105)

There's an old belief that bears always catch fish by slapping them out of the water with a paw. But this isn't true. A grizzly bear usually fishes by wading into a stream and snatching up a fish in its mouth—just as the one in these pictures is doing.

The Sonoran pronghorn

The pronghorn is special in two ways.

First, it is probably the fastest large animal in North or South America. When a pronghorn is only four days old it can run faster than a human being. And a full-grown pronghorn can run more than sixty miles an hour for short distances! That's about as fast as most cars go on a main highway.

Second, there is no other animal quite like a pronghorn. Although it is often called the American antelope, it is not really an antelope. The pronghorn is a one-of-a-kind creature that lives only in North America. But there are different kinds of pronghorns. It is the Sonoran pronghorn that is in danger. There are only about a thousand of them left.

Sonoran pronghorns live on the desert in a small part of Mexico and a small part of Arizona. They are little animals, only about three and one-half feet high at the shoulder. They roam about in bands of from five to twenty-five during summer. But in winter they gather in large herds of a hundred or more. Day and night, most of their time is spent in eating. Their food is grass and small plants.

For a long time, the Sonoran pronghorns were hunted. People also took over much of the land where the pronghorns lived. Sheep and horses now graze on the land. These animals eat much of the food the pronghorns need. Without enough food, the Sonoran pronghorns may not be able to survive much longer.

The California condor

The body of a dead sheep lay in a grassy meadow on a mountainside. Two jet-black ravens perched on the body, tearing bits of flesh from it.

Suddenly, a great shadow glided over the body. Overhead, a big bird soared on wings that stretched more than nine feet from tip to tip. Slowly, the bird circled down and landed a short distance from the dead sheep. With its wings held partly out for balance, it waddled to the body.

At once, the ravens flew away. The big bird bent

over the sheep. With its sharp, curved beak, it hungrily
ripped off chunks of meat. This bird, a California
condor, is one of the largest flying birds in the
world. It feeds chiefly on the flesh of dead animals.

California condors spend much of their time sitting
in the sun on branches of dead trees or on rocky
cliff tops. They often bathe in nearby streams. When
they get hungry, they fly over the countryside
looking for the bodies of dead cattle, sheep, deer,
or other big animals. When a condor drops down out of
the sky to eat, most other birds that may be eating
already will quickly get out of its way. But condors
share their finds with each other.

The California condor once lived in most of western
North America. Now, there are only about forty of
these big birds left. They all live in a sanctuary in
Los Padres National Forest in southern California.
They are protected by law, but even so they are
sometimes shot.

The American alligator

American alligators live in swamps and marshes in the southeastern United States. These big reptiles have long tails, round noses, and scaly, tough-skinned bodies. They sometimes grow to be twelve feet long.

During the day, alligators lie in warm, sunny places or float like logs in pools of blue-green water. At night, they hunt. They eat fish, frogs, snakes, turtles, muskrats, and even smaller alligators.

Snakes, turtles, lizards, and most other members of the reptile family are very quiet. Alligators are the noisy members of the family. Baby alligators grunt like pigs. Grown male alligators bellow like bulls, and in the spring their roaring fills the swamps.

Alligators are very useful animals. They tear up thick patches of jungle to make holes for themselves. The holes fill up with swamp water and become ponds where fish, water birds, and other animals can live. And alligators actually help keep the water full of fish by eating turtles that eat many kinds of fish. An alligator plays a very important part in the natural life of the place where it lives.

But many people are afraid of alligators. They try to kill them whenever they can. Alligators are also hunted for their skins, which are made into shoes, belts, purses, and suitcases. There used to be millions of American alligators. Today, there are only thousands. Even though they are now protected by law, they are slowly being wiped out. These big reptiles may soon be gone from the wild forever.

The Texas ocelot

The ocelot looks like it is part tiger and part leopard. It has spots and rings like a leopard, and short stripes somewhat like those of a tiger. In Texas, the ocelot is sometimes called a leopard cat. In Mexico, it is often called a tiger cat. It may look like both a leopard and a tiger, but it isn't as big as either. It's about twice as big as a house cat.

Ocelots are forest animals. They spend much of their time in trees. They can leap about in the branches with great skill, but they can also run very fast on the ground. During the day, an ocelot may doze in a leafy tree, out of the sunlight. At night, it comes down to hunt for rats, mice, snakes, lizards, turtles, frogs, and small birds.

The Texas ocelot used to live in many parts of the southern United States and northern Mexico. But people have pushed it out. Now this ocelot is found only in a small part of Texas and a few parts of Mexico. And it is in danger because people hunt it for its beautiful fur.

The bald eagle

The bald eagle isn't really bald. Its head is thickly covered with white feathers. Long ago, when this eagle was named, the word "bald" meant "white."

The bald eagle is a hunter—a bird of prey. It soars through the sky, its sharp, fierce eyes alert for any movement on the ground below. When it spies a small animal such as a rabbit or ground squirrel, it swoops down. Gliding close to the ground, it seizes the animal in its long, curved talons. The eagle also catches small birds and fish the same way.

When a male and female bald eagle choose each other as mates, they stay together for life. Together, they build an enormous nest of sticks and grass. This nest is always high above the ground, often in a dead pine tree. The mother eagle usually lays two eggs. The parents take turns sitting on the eggs and hunting food for the baby eagles when they hatch.

Although bald eagles are protected by law, many of them have been shot by farmers and ranchers who believe the eagles attack lambs and calves. The bald eagle is also in trouble because of poisons in our lakes and rivers. These poisons get into the eagles' bodies when they eat fish. The poisons then cause the eagles to lay spoiled eggs, so that fewer and fewer baby eagles are hatched.

The bald eagle is the emblem of the United States. You can see its picture on dollar bills, on coins, and many other places. But you can no longer see many of the eagles themselves. They are dying out and may soon be extinct.

South America

The river turtle

For weeks, a steady rain has poured down from a dark sky. It rattles on the leaves of plants and hisses into the broad, gray river. So much rain has fallen, the river is overflowing its banks. Much of the land on both sides of the river is already under water.

Thousands of huge turtles live in the watery, muddy land near the river. These big turtles have round shells up to two or three feet wide and move very slowly. They constantly search for fruits, flowers, and soft, leafy plants to eat.

At last, the rain begins to let up. The rainy season

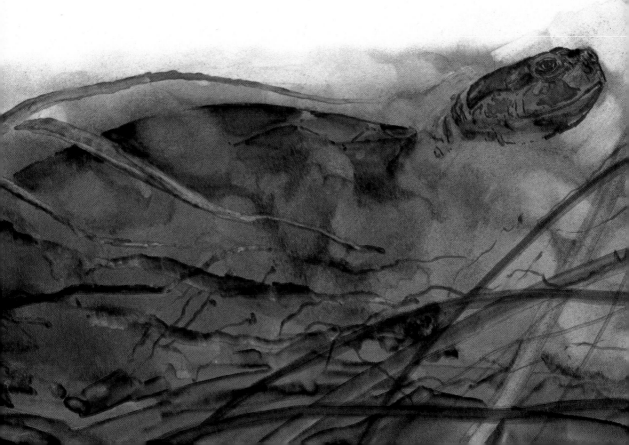

is ending. When the rain does stop, the hot, tropical sun comes out again. Slowly, the water in the river begins to go down.

Now the turtles stop eating and head for the river. Soon, the water is filled with turtles, all swimming in the same direction. Often they must battle against strong currents and make their way through rushing rapids. But nothing stops them. They swim on until they reach their goal—some little islands in the river. Each year, this is where they mate and lay their eggs.

For several days, the female turtles lie on the beach, at the water's edge, basking in the hot sun. Then, one night, they all begin to crawl farther up on the beach to lay their eggs. The beach is covered with turtles, each one looking for just the right place.

When a turtle decides she has found the right place, she digs a hole in the sand. This hole is as wide as she is. She may lay eighty or more round, soft-shelled eggs in the hole. Then she covers the eggs, carefully smoothing out the sand so that there is no sign of the nest. When this is done, the mother turtle crawls back down to the river and swims away.

Day after day, the hot sun bakes down on the sand. About forty-five days after the eggs are laid, the tiny baby turtles begin to hatch. They dig their way up out of the sand. Soon the beach is covered with tiny, scurrying shapes. Thousands of baby turtles are rushing down to the water. But many of them never make it. Swarms of vultures and other birds swoop down to gobble up the little turtles. Even when the babies reach the water, they aren't safe. Crocodiles

and fish wait to eat as many as they can.

These turtles have lived in the Orinoco and Amazon rivers of South America for millions of years. Many baby turtles were eaten each year, but enough got away so that there were always a great many turtles.

At least there used to be. And there still would be, if it weren't for people. But for several hundred years, people have come to the islands and taken millions of turtle eggs before they could hatch. Now, there are many places where there are no turtles. After millions of years, the South American river turtles are in danger of becoming extinct—because of people.

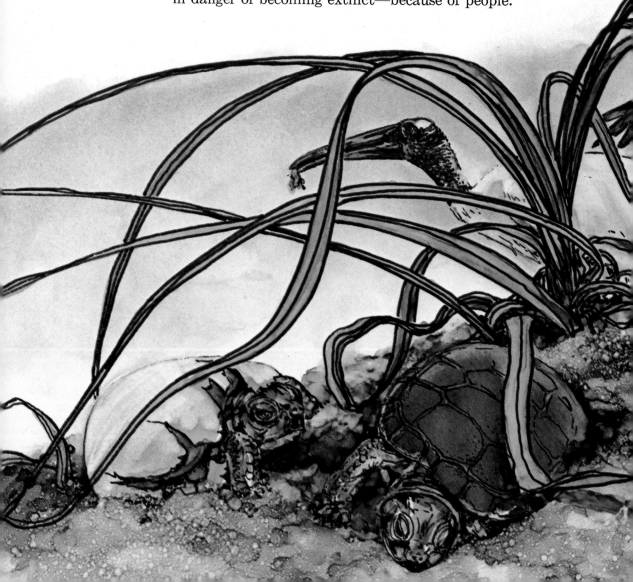

The red uakari

A uakari always looks sad. It isn't, of course—that's just the way it looks to us. Most of the time a uakari is rather quiet. This, too, makes it seem sad. But when it becomes excited, it lets out loud yells. And when a uakari is excited, its pink face turns bright red.

Uakaris are little monkeys, about a foot and one half long not counting their short tails. They are slim creatures, but their shaggy fur makes them look rather chubby. The fur protects them from the heavy rains that fall on their hot, wet, rain forest home near the Amazon River.

Uakaris live in the tops of trees. Active, skillful climbers, they hardly ever come down to the ground. They live together in little bands. During the day they scurry about in search of food. They eat fruits, nuts, and leaves, as well as small birds, lizards, tree frogs, and other small animals.

These little, sad-faced monkeys are in grave danger. Their forest home is being cut down and they are being hunted. No one knows just how many uakaris there are, but there are not many.

The giant armadillo

The giant armadillo waddled along the sandy riverbank. It was searching for a place to dig itself a shelter. From time to time it reared up slightly to walk on its two back legs, with its front legs hanging down and barely touching the ground.

When the armadillo found a good spot, it began to dig. It was a wonderfully fast and skillful digger. Sand flew, and the hole grew quickly. As it dug, the armadillo uncovered a plump, wiggly worm, or a juicy insect. Then it had a quick snack. It would also gladly have eaten any snakes or spiders it found.

From the tip of its nose to the end of its tail, the giant armadillo is about five feet long. It weighs more than 130 pounds. The big, sharp claws on its front feet are perfect for digging.

With its strong claws and shell of bumpy, bony armor, the giant armadillo looks like a fierce creature that can take good care of itself. But this big animal is really quite timid. If an enemy appears, the armadillo tries to run away rather than fight. And if

it can't get away, it curls up in a ball and depends upon its thick skin and bony armor to save it.

There are not very many of these curious-looking, armorplated animals. The forests where they live are being cleared, and sometimes they are hunted. Scientists fear that the giant armadillo is slowly being wiped out.

The chinchilla

The chinchilla is a member of the rat family—a rat with the finest fur in the world! A little, mouselike creature, it is about a foot long and has a ten-inch, bushy tail. Its thick fur is so fine and silky that a coat made of chinchilla fur has sold for as much as $100,000!

Chinchillas need their thick fur to keep warm. They live high up in the snow-capped Andes Mountains. Little family groups of from two to five animals share burrows among the rocks. They sleep during the day and come out at night. Then they hop and scurry in search of grass, seeds, roots, moss, and any other plant food they can find. When a chinchilla eats, it sits up on its hind legs and tail, like a squirrel, and holds its food in its front paws.

The Spaniards who came to South America five hundred years ago named the chinchilla after the Chincha Indians. Because of their beautiful fur, chinchillas were nearly wiped out by hunters and trappers. For many years, scientists thought chinchillas were extinct. Then a few were found and captured. These captives were the ancestors of thousands of chinchillas that are now raised on special ranches.

Because there are so many ranch chinchillas, the chinchilla family will probably never die out. But the wild chinchillas are still in great trouble. Their fur is finer than the fur of the ranch chinchillas, so people still hunt and trap them. The wild chinchillas may not be able to survive much longer.

The spectacled bear

It's easy to see how the spectacled bear got its name. The circles of yellowish fur around its eyes make it look as if it is wearing a pair of enormous spectacles.

The spectacled bear is the only kind of wild bear that lives in South America. It is a small bear, about five feet long and a little more than two feet high. It lives in forests on the slopes of mountains. Not very much is known about the spectacled bear. It seems to be more of a plant-eater than other bears, living mostly on leaves, fruits, and roots.

Like most bears, the spectacled bear is a skillful climber. It sometimes stands upright, to pull leafy branches down to its mouth, but it often climbs trees for its food. It is fond of the leaves of a certain kind of palm tree. It climbs the tree, tears off branches, and lets them fall to the ground. Then it climbs down and eats the leaves off the branches. Some people think that spectacled bears build nests of twigs and branches, high in trees.

The spectacled bear is slowly disappearing. People hunt it and set traps for it. There may be only a few thousand of these animals left.

The maned wolf

The maned wolf is sometimes called the "fox that walks on stilts." Its long legs may look strange, but they help this animal to run very fast.

Not much is known about maned wolves because they prefer to stay away from people. Maned wolves live by themselves on grassy plains and at the edges of swampy forests. They sleep during the day and come out at night to hunt. They eat mostly rats and mice, but will hunt birds, lizards, and other small animals. They also like fruit and insects. Maned wolves that have been caught and put in zoos are usually smart, playful, and friendly.

There are probably only a few thousand of these long-legged creatures. They seem to be in trouble, but no one is sure why. The wolves are not hunted much. They have not lost too much of their land. Still, they are disappearing. Scientists want to study them to find out why this is happening and if they can be saved.

The giant otter

Mosquitoes hummed and dragonflies darted above the water of a quiet stream. Just below the surface of the water, a fat, silver-scaled fish waited for one of the insects to come near enough to be caught.

But the fish wasn't to have dinner—it was going to *be* dinner! Behind it, a big, chocolate-brown animal glided silently through the water. Bright eyes in a blunt, whiskery face watched the fish. A hungry giant otter!

There was an explosion of bubbles as the otter rushed at the fish. With a desperate flick of its tail, the fish dived for the bottom, trying to escape. But it couldn't get away. Sharp teeth clamped onto its body.

With the fish in its mouth, the otter swam to the shore. Leaving the water, it climbed up the bank, wriggling its way over a bump, just like a seal. Shaking itself briskly, it sent a shower of water in all directions. Then it began to devour the fish.

The giant otter is truly a giant. From its blunt nose to the end of its long, flat tail, it measures six feet. Giant otters live in holes in the banks of quiet creeks and streams. They spend much of their time in the water and are fine swimmers. When a giant otter moves through the water, it looks almost like a big fish.

A great hunter, the giant otter eats fish, shellfish, birds, and small animals. But it, in turn, is also hunted—not for food but for its rich, beautiful brown fur. Because they have been hunted so much, there are very few giant otters left.

mother anteater with a baby on her back

The giant anteater

Beneath a tree in a swampy forest, a giant anteater lay sleeping. Curled into a ball, it was completely covered by its enormous, bushy tail.

The anteater awoke as the morning sun rose in the sky and the forest grew lighter. When the animal uncurled itself and stood up, it was more than six feet long. Slowly, the anteater ambled off into the forest, nose close to the ground. To protect its big, curling claws, it walked on the knuckles of its front feet.

The anteater lumbered through the forest. Once, it passed a female anteater carrying a baby on her back. The two grown-up anteaters did not stay together, however. Anteaters prefer to be by themselves most of the time.

The anteater soon came to the edge of the forest. Ahead of it, on the plain, it saw something that looked like a tall, pointed rock. But this was no rock—it was a termite nest made of rock-hard clay. The anteater hurried toward it.

The hard clay was no match for the anteater's claws. The animal quickly tore the nest apart. Termites scurried in all directions. Out of the anteater's mouth flowed a long, sticky, tongue. It began to lick up termites by the dozens.

With its long, pointed head and great, bushy tail, the giant anteater is an odd-looking creature. Sadly, it may soon be extinct. This harmless, slow-moving animal is easy to hunt. So many people have hunted it just for "fun" that there are few giant anteaters left.

The golden lion marmoset

Golden lion marmosets are tiny, beautiful monkeys. Their gleaming, yellow-gold fur is long and silky. Lionlike manes surround their little faces. Only about ten inches long, golden lion marmosets have fluffy tails that are longer than they are.

These tiny creatures live in thick forests. Quick-moving and active, they dart and scurry and leap from branch to branch like golden blurs. They are also noisy, squeaking and chattering most of the time. They travel together in groups, searching for fruits, insects, tiny lizards, and small birds. When marmosets want to sleep or rest, they usually hide in the hollow of a tree.

Male golden lion marmosets make fine fathers. They carry the babies on their backs and help to feed them when they are old enough for solid food. A marmoset father squeezes bits of food between his fingers to make it soft before he gives it to his youngster. Even when a young marmoset is able to take care of itself, its father often seems to want to look after it!

There are probably less than a thousand of these beautiful little animals. The forest where they live is being cut down to make room for sugar, coffee, and banana plantations. The marmosets are being pushed out of their home. They are also caught and sold as pets. If something isn't done soon, they will become extinct.

The vicuña

Camels are rather ugly creatures. But the vicuña, which belongs to the camel family, is a beautiful animal. This dainty, graceful little beast is about three feet high at the shoulder. Its golden-brown wool is like fine, soft silk.

Vicuñas live in a brown, treeless land high in the Andes Mountains, where the air is thin and cold. They travel about in small, family herds of from six to fifteen animals—a leader and his wives and young ones. While the herd feeds on grass and small

plants, the leader stands guard over them. If danger approaches, the leader makes a whistling noise. Then the females and young ones hurry away. The leader bravely puts himself between them and the enemy.

Five hundred years ago the Inca Indians protected vicuñas. They hunted them only once every four years. Only the Inca kings could use the vicuña's beautiful, silky wool. The vicuña is still protected. But a coat made of vicuña wool is worth a great deal of money. That's why hundreds of thousands of vicuñas have been killed by law-breaking hunters. Now, there are probably less than twenty thousand of these graceful, beautiful little animals.

The quetzal

The bright splash of green on the trunk of the dead tree was an air plant—a plant that grows on a tree. Its long, feathery leaves hung down toward the ground.

But some of the leaves weren't leaves at all—they were feathers! A bird was snuggled into a hole in the trunk, with its long, green tail feathers hanging down among the leaves. The feathers looked so much like the leaves that the bird was completely hidden.

The bird slipped out of its nest and flew off. Its three-foot-long tail feathers streamed out behind it. Its green body sparkled like an emerald and its red breast glowed like a ruby.

For hundreds of years, the people of Central America have admired this beautiful bird. It is called a quetzal. In the language of the ancient Aztecs, this means "tail feather." The Aztecs also used the word to mean anything precious or beautiful.

Only male quetzals have the long tail feathers. Females do not have them. These birds live in the upper parts of tall trees in rain forests. They hardly ever come down to the ground. They drink raindrops that fall on leaves. They eat fruits and insects they find in the trees.

Because the quetzal is so beautiful, it has long been hunted for its feathers. It is also losing its forest home, which is being chopped down and turned into farmland. So the quetzal, one of the most beautiful birds in the world, is in danger of becoming extinct.

Australia

The red kangaroo

Stars twinkle and a bright full moon glows above a grassy, rolling plain. Far in the distance, there is the shrill cry of a bird.

A "mob," or herd, of several dozen kangaroos is feeding on the grass that grows on the plain. They are large animals. Some of the reddish-colored males are nearly seven feet tall when they stand up straight and balance themselves with their tails. The smaller females are a smoky-blue color. These females are dainty, graceful creatures. They are sometimes called "blue flyers." Many of the females are carrying babies, called "joeys." Their bright eyes peer out from their mothers' pouches.

The kangaroos move about slowly, in little hops. They put their front paws and tails on the ground, then

give a jump with their back legs. They look as if they are playing leapfrog. Many of the kangaroos keep all four feet on the ground while they eat. When they finish eating, they lick their paws and rub them on their fur, just as cats do.

Through the rest of the night, and into the early morning, the kangaroos keep grazing. Then, as the plain begins to heat up under the glare of the sun, the kangaroos stop eating. They follow their leader, a big male, to the shade of a tiny clump of trees. Here they will rest during the heat of the day.

Many of the kangaroos lie down on their sides and go to sleep. Others simply stretch out contentedly in the shade. But some of the young kangaroos want to play! Two of them start to box. They rise up on their toes and balance on their tails. Holding their front paws near their chests, they duck and jab and punch at each

other, just like two prize fighters. Then, one jumps up
in the air and kicks the other in the stomach with both
hind feet! That ends the fight.

After a time, all of the kangaroos, young and old,
settle down to rest. Suddenly, a female raises her head.
Rising to her full height, she stares out across the
plain. Something is coming!

In an instant, the whole mob is bounding away,

sailing through the air in tremendous twenty-five-foot
jumps. Traveling at nearly thirty miles an hour, they
are soon out of sight.

Many people are worried about the red kangaroo,
and its cousin, the gray kangaroo. Millions of kangaroos
have been killed by hunters each year. The meat was
sold to companies that make pet food. Some sheep
and cattle owners shoot and poison kangaroos, because
the kangaroos eat grass that the sheep and cattle need.

There are no longer as many kangaroos as there once
were. Many people fear that these marvelous jumpers
may someday become extinct.

The rabbit-eared bandicoot

A rabbit-eared bandicoot lay sleeping in a burrow it had dug in the sandy earth. The bandicoot had a long, pointed nose and was about the size of a cat. But it looked like a mouse with the ears of a rabbit. It was a female, and had a pouch on its stomach in which to carry its babies.

The bandicoot did not sleep lying down. It sat on its tail, with its head bent forward and its nose tucked between its front paws. Its long ears were stretched forward to cover its eyes.

The burrow in which the bandicoot slept was at the end of a long, winding tunnel. This tunnel went nearly six feet deep into the earth. With dirt and darkness around it, the bandicoot was protected from the terrible heat of the sun that baked the dry, brown plain during the day.

The sun sank lower in the sky and finally disappeared over the horizon. Darkness flowed over the plain. After a while, the bandicoot stirred and woke up. It scrambled out of the burrow and trotted gracefully off into the night. It held its long, black and white tail up like a flag.

Coming to a clump of bushes, the little animal began to dig and scratch in the dirt. Its work was rewarded, for among the roots it found some plump caterpillars to eat. Perhaps, later, it would be lucky enough to find some of its favorite food—termites.

Fewer and fewer rabbit-eared bandicoots are seen in Australia. For years they were hunted for their long, silky fur. Some were killed by traps set for rabbits, and many others by foxes brought to Australia from Europe. These little creatures may be dying out.

The hairy-nosed wombat

Some people think it looks like a beaver without a tail. Others say it looks like a badger. But it really doesn't look quite like either one. It looks like—well, a wombat. This pudgy, short-legged, snub-nosed creature is about three feet long. It has a tiny stump of a tail that can hardly be seen. And, like most other Australian animals, a wombat has a pouch in which to carry its babies.

The hairy-nosed wombat is an expert digger. It lies on its side and digs with the strong, curved claws on all four of its feet. It likes to make long, long tunnels in soft soil beneath cliffs and boulders. At the end of the tunnel it makes a large nest of leaves and bark. There it sleeps during the day, coming out at night to eat grass and roots.

Wombats are in trouble mainly because of rabbits. Rabbits are not native to Australia. Once there were no rabbits at all. Then some were brought from Europe so people could hunt them. At that time, Australia had few animals that hunt rabbits and help to keep their numbers down. So the number of rabbits grew tremendously.

Now there are probably thousands of rabbits to each wombat. The rabbits eat the wombats' food and take over the wombats' burrows. And when farmers use poison to kill rabbits, wombats are often poisoned, too. Wombats are also shot and trapped because they tear holes in fences put up to keep rabbits out. As a result, the wombats are fast disappearing.

The Tasmanian wolf

The Tasmanian wolf, or Tasmanian tiger as it is called in Australia, is neither a wolf nor a tiger. It's an animal that has a head like a wolf, a tail like a dog, stripes like a tiger, and a pouch like a kangaroo! Scientists call it a thylacine—a word that means "pouched dog with a wolf's head."

Tasmanian wolves are about three feet long—slightly larger than a fox. Forest dwellers, they live in rocky dens or hollow logs. They sometimes lie about in the sun during the day, but they are night animals. They hunt after dark, often in small groups. Kangaroos, wallabies, and small birds and animals are their prey.

There are probably very, very few Tasmanian wolves left. Once there were many of these animals on the island of Tasmania, which is part of Australia. But people tried to wipe them out because the wolves sometimes killed sheep and chickens. Most of the wolves were killed off—no one has seen a Tasmanian wolf for more than thirty years. Scientists think some are still alive, because their tracks and dens have been found. But the wolf that isn't a wolf is very close to becoming extinct.

The ring-tailed rock wallaby

Wallabies look like midget kangaroos. Female wallabies carry their babies in pouches, just as female kangaroos do.

The ring-tailed rock wallaby gets its name from its furry-tipped tail, which is striped with brown and yellow rings. This wallaby lives in caves in rocky, hilly parts of Australia. You can always tell when many wallabies have lived in a cave. The rock floor of the cave will be polished as smooth as marble. The bottoms of a rock wallaby's feet are like rough sandpaper. As the wallabies walk around in a cave, their feet smooth and polish the floor.

A ring-tailed rock wallaby sleeps in its cave most of the day. It may come out to enjoy the sun on warm afternoons, but nighttime is when it is really active. That's when it hops about in search of the tasty grass, juicy tree bark, and roots that are its food. If it meets an enemy, it hops away in great twelve-foot leaps. It may even climb a tree or scramble up the side of a steep cliff to safety.

The ring-tailed rock wallaby may be in trouble. There are not many of these creatures, and they are hunted for their fur. They are no longer seen in many of the places where they used to live.

Europe

The peregrine falcon

High above the shining surface of a lake in Scotland, a black speck wheels slowly in the sky. Higher still, a second speck flies above the first. The specks are a male and female peregrine falcon, hunting.

The male, called a tiercel, is the scout for the pair. His larger and stronger mate flies above him. She waits to have the first try at any unwary bird the two falcons may see. If she misses, the tiercel will swoop at it next.

From the edge of the lake, a young dunlin takes wing, flapping up into the sky. It has not seen the circling specks above it—and it is doomed.

The female falcon hurls herself into a dive. Her wings go straight back and close halfway, flickering rapidly to pick up speed. In seconds she is falling like a stone, diving so fast the air hisses past her. She is traveling nearly 175 miles an hour!

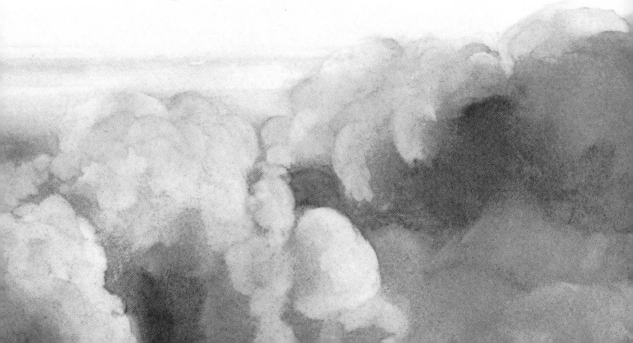

Coming out of her power dive, the falcon swoops
alongside the little dunlin. At the last instant the dunlin
sees her and tries to turn aside. But it cannot escape
this swift, skilled hunter of the skies. The falcon thrusts
out one foot and snatches the dunlin in mid-air.
Caught in the murderous, crushing grip of the falcon's
curved, razor-sharp talons, the little dunlin is killed
almost instantly.

With the lifeless body of the dunlin dangling from
her claws, the falcon sweeps around in a great curve.
She and her mate head back toward a line of gray cliffs
rising in the distance.

The falcons' nest is on a narrow ledge high up on one of the cliffs. It is not a nest such as most kinds of birds make. Using her beak and claws, the falcon just scratched a shallow circle about an inch deep. Here, about a month before, she had hatched three eggs.

The baby falcons waiting in the nest peer hungrily at the sky. Their sharp eyes see their mother when she is no more than a tiny dot in the distance. They begin to hop and flap their wings, screaming shrilly.

As if to tease her youngsters, the mother falcon flies right past the nest. Perhaps she is just making sure

that there are no enemies nearby. But, moments later, she rushes back to swoop down and drop the dunlin on the ledge.

Now there is a fight. The young birds scramble for the prize. After a few moments, one of the youngsters pulls the dunlin away from the others. He covers the dead bird with his wings and body so the others can't get at it. The others must wait until their mother or father brings back another bird.

When the young falcons are a little older, and able to fly, their parents will drop food beyond the ledge. Then

the young ones will have to catch it in mid-air. In this way the young falcons will learn how to catch flying birds. They will soon become as good hunters as their parents.

For hundreds of years people have admired the marvelous flying and hunting skill of peregrine falcons. In the days of knights and castles, most kings and nobles kept pet falcons. These birds were trained to bring back the birds or animals they caught. Hunting with trained falcons was a popular sport called falconry. There are many people who still train falcons and hunt with them today.

The peregrine falcon lives throughout Europe and parts of North America. It is in great trouble almost everywhere. Many of the birds it eats have been poisoned by chemicals. This poison comes from sprays that farmers use to kill insects. The poison has seeped into lakes, ponds, and rivers everywhere in the world. It gets into birds' bodies when they eat fish. Then it gets into falcons' bodies when they catch and eat the birds.

The poison causes the female falcons to lay eggs that have very thin shells. The shells often break before the baby birds inside are ready to hatch. Then the babies die. This means that fewer and fewer babies hatch each year.

Many scientists fear that if our waters are not cleaned up soon, nothing can be done for the peregrine falcon. These wonderful flying hunters may all be gone from the world in twenty or thirty years.

The Spanish lynx

The lynx is a cousin of the lion, tiger, leopard, and jaguar. But it is a cat with a special sort of look. Most cats have rounded ears and long tails. But a lynx's ears come to sharp points and have spikes of fur on the tips. And instead of being long, a lynx's tail is short and stubby. Thick whiskers hang from a lynx's cheeks. Its head looks too small for its three-foot-long body, and its feet seem much too big.

The Spanish lynx is a forest animal. It prowls among

the trees, after dark, hunting for rabbits and other small animals and birds. The lynx is a fast, fierce hunter that can climb trees easily and swim well. It has large, fluffy feet that help it move quickly and easily over thick snow.

Spanish lynxes once lived almost everywhere in Spain. But most of the forests where they lived have been cut down. Because the lynxes sometimes killed sheep and other farm animals, people hunted them and nearly killed them all. Today, only a few hundred of these handsome cats are left. They are scattered about in the few wild places left in Spain.

The Mediterranean monk seal

Most seals are cold-water creatures that live in icy northern seas. But the small, dark-brown seals called monk seals like warm places. For many thousands of years they have lived in the warm waters of the Mediterranean, Adriatic, and Black seas. Small groups of monk seals often stay in rocky caves on islands and beaches.

The ancient Greeks and Romans seem to have liked these seals. Greek and Roman poets wrote about them. The Greeks even put pictures of the monk seal on some of their coins.

But this was long ago, when not many people lived in that part of the world. As time went by, there were more and more people. Many of these people fished for a living. And fishing is how the monk seals make *their* living, for they are fish-eaters.

Most fishermen soon felt there were too many monk seals, eating too many fish. So the fishermen began a war on the seals—a war that has been going on for hundreds of years. They simply killed every monk seal they saw.

Today, there are very few monk seals left. There are not enough of them to eat many fish, but fishermen still kill them. Unless this can be stopped, the Mediterranean monk seal will surely become extinct.

The Arctic

The Atlantic walrus

Sunlight sparkled on the calm waters of the Arctic Ocean. The air was bitter cold, and white, floating islands of ice dotted the blue water.

One of these ice floes was covered with big, reddish-brown animals. A herd of walruses dozed and sunned upon it. Several dozen of the big creatures snuggled together, sometimes even lying one on top of another. There were huge males, smaller females, and young pups snoozing beside their mothers.

The full-grown males were enormous animals. Many of them were as much as twelve feet long and weighed nearly three thousand pounds. They had thick, wrinkled, bumpy skin, and tusks almost three feet long. Some of the older males had tusks that had been broken in fights. Others had worn their tusks down to stumps. Walruses use their tusks to pull themselves up onto the ice. The tusks slowly wear down from this kind of use.

One of the big males decided he was hungry. Rearing up on his flippers, he waddled over the ice toward the water, bumping and pushing the others in his path. There were angry, elephantlike bellows from some of them as their rest was disturbed. The big male slipped easily into the water and dived straight down, more than two hundred feet, to the ocean floor. Here there were beds of clams from which the walruses got most of their food.

After a time, his stomach now comfortably full of clams, the walrus popped up to the surface. Slowly, he swam back to the ice floe. Stretching his head out of the water, he slammed the points of his tusks into the ice. He then pulled his huge weight up onto the floe. Now he was ready to go to sleep again.

But he paused, staring out across the blue, sparkling water. Something was moving swiftly toward the ice floe. Several of the other walruses saw it too, and reared up for a better look.

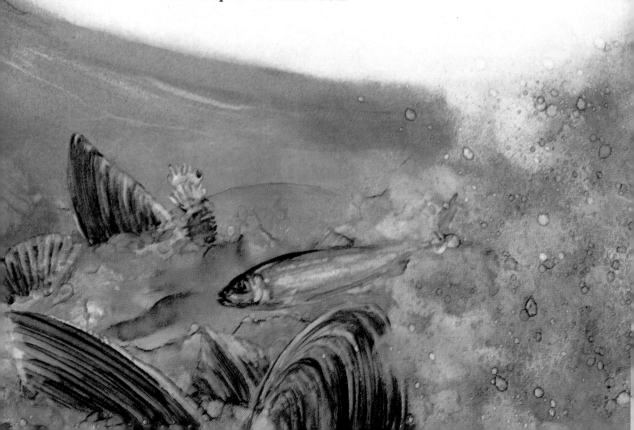

Suddenly, the sharp crack of a rifle shot split the cold, quiet air! A male walrus who had raised himself up to stare, dropped to the ice with a thud. He lay still, bright blood oozing from a bullet hole in his body.

Instantly, the entire herd rushed for the water. Males bellowed and females anxiously pushed their babies to make them hurry. The enemy had come!

The enemy was a group of Eskimo hunters in a boat. Eskimos have hunted walruses for thousands of years. They could usually kill enough animals for their needs. But with only spears and harpoons, they were never able to kill too many.

Then, people from other lands came with guns. They were able to kill many more walruses than the Eskimos could. Because of all this hunting, there are not many Atlantic walruses left.

Today, only Eskimos are allowed to hunt walruses. But Eskimos now have guns, too. They can kill many more walruses than they ever could before. The Eskimos have to hunt walruses. They still depend upon these animals for many of their needs. But scientists fear that if many more walruses are killed, these big animals will soon become extinct. Then the Eskimos may suffer.

The polar bear

The world of the polar bear is the frozen Arctic region around the North Pole. Here, these big, white giants roam alone over vast fields of snow-covered ice. Very good swimmers, they often ride ice floes across hundreds of miles of open ocean.

Most polar bears stay on the move all year long. But females with babies stay in dens during the winter. Before the dark, winter days begin, the female digs a deep hole in the snow. Down in this snowy cave, her cubs are born. Mother and babies spend the winter months cuddled together. The mother dozes most of the time. She does not eat at all, but lives on the stored-up fat in her body. The cubs live on her milk.

While mothers and cubs stay in their winter dens, other polar bears roam through the cold darkness. They search for holes in the ice that show where seals are. The seals swimming below the ice make these holes so they can come up to fill their lungs with air. A polar bear will wait for hours at one of these breathing holes. When a seal pops its head up, the bear scoops the seal out of the water with one swipe of its mighty paw.

Although polar bears will eat roots, berries, and plants in spring and summer, they are mostly meat-eaters. In fact, they are one of the biggest of all meat-eating animals. A full-grown male polar bear is usually about seven or eight feet long and five feet high. Some are even more than twelve feet long.

In recent years, people started hunting polar bears from power boats and airplanes. Far too many bears were killed. So it is now against the law to hunt them. But not many of these big, lonely wanderers are left.

Oceans and Islands

The southern sea otter

Down among the rocks and seaweed on the ocean floor, a sea otter searched for something to eat. Red and yellow starfish moved slowly among the rocks, but the otter wasn't much interested in them. They weren't very tasty. What the otter really wanted was a nice, plump sea urchin, a clam or an oyster, a fat fish, or —best of all—an abalone.

Oh! The otter's sharp eyes saw a cluster of oysters huddled together on a boulder. In an instant, she scooped up two of them and tucked them under one of her front legs. Then she picked up a flat rock that lay in the sand. She tucked it under her other front leg.

With a whip of her flipper-shaped back feet, the otter shot up to the surface of the water. Popping out into the air, she rolled over onto her back and began

to float. It was lunchtime. First, she put the flat rock on her chest. Then, taking one of the oysters between her paws, she smashed it down against the rock. After several whacks, the oyster cracked open. The otter happily gobbled up the soft, whitish meat inside the shell.

When she finished eating, she rolled over in the water to wash away scraps of food stuck to her fur. It is very important for a sea otter to keep its fur clean. The thick, brown fur traps a blanket of air all around the otter's body. This air helps the otter to float. It also protects the otter against cold. If the fur gets dirty, or is stuck together, the otter cannot float. It may also die from the cold. So otters spend lots of time cleaning their fur.

Otters also spend lots of time eating. A full-grown otter, which may be four feet long, can eat more than fifteen pounds of food a day. That's a lot more than you eat! Sea otters get most of their food by diving down to the ocean floor. They usually stay down about

a minute and a half. But they can stay down as long as four minutes if they have to.

A mother otter usually has only one baby each time she gives birth. The mother and baby stay together for about a year. The baby spends most of its time lying on its mother's chest, while she floats on her back. When the mother gets hungry, she pushes the baby into the water. While she dives down for food, the baby floats like a cork. Sometimes the mother wraps seaweed around the baby to keep it from floating too far away. Sea otters often wrap themselves in seaweed when they sleep, so they won't float too far from the place where they get their food.

Southern sea otters live in shallow water off parts of the coast of California. There used to be thousands of them. But they were hunted for their fur, until they were nearly all gone. They are now in trouble because of water pollution, which gets their fur dirty and oily. The otters are also in trouble because abalone fishermen kill them to protect the abalone. Unless we can find ways to help them, the southern sea otters could easily become extinct.

The Galapagos penguin

When sailors from Europe first saw penguins, they thought they were fish with feathers. And penguins certainly act as if they are half bird and half fish.

On land, Galapagos penguins behave like birds. They sit for hours on rocky beaches that they share with small lizards. They constantly peer about with bright, bird eyes. When they want to go somewhere, they move with little hops, holding their feet together.

But when Galapagos penguins go into the water to hunt for the small fish they eat, they seem to be fish themselves. They shoot through the water with little

flicks of their flippery wings. They dive in and out
of the waves like porpoises at play!

Penguins live in the southern half of the world. Most
kinds are found near the South Pole, or at the bottom
of South America, Africa, and Australia. But the
Galapagos penguin lives in the *middle* of the world. It
is found only on the Galapagos Islands.

The Galapagos Islands are in the Pacific Ocean, off
the coast of South America. There are fifteen of these
islands, and they are right on the equator. The little
penguins once lived on all of the islands. But many of
the birds were killed by people and the eggs stolen for
food. Now, only a few thousand Galapagos penguins are
left, and they live on only two of the islands.

The blue whale

The surface of the ocean is calm and quiet. Suddenly, an enormous, bluish-gray body pushes up out of the water! A thick spout of steam hisses a dozen feet into the air. A blue whale has come up to "blow."

Whales look like giant fish, but they are really mammals—like dogs, cows, horses, and humans. They cannot breathe under water. A blue whale can hold its breath under water for about twenty minutes. The air in its lungs gets hot and steamy. When the whale surfaces, it blows the air out through two holes in the top of its head. This hot air makes a great fountain of steam when it shoots out into the cold, ocean air.

The blue whale is the biggest of all animals. A full-grown blue whale may be nearly a hundred feet long and weigh 300,000 pounds—that's bigger and heavier than the biggest dinosaur that ever lived! In fact, when a blue whale is born, it is *already* bigger than a full-grown elephant!

In summer, blue whales stay in cold water near the North or South poles. In winter, they move into warmer parts of the ocean. They travel alone, or in pairs, following the huge clouds of tiny shrimplike creatures called krill that drift in the ocean. A blue whale eats thousands of pounds of these creatures each day. To eat, a whale just swims into a crowd of krill with its mouth open. As the whale closes its mouth, its tongue pushes the water out. This leaves only the krill, which the whale then swallows.

Blue whales have been hunted until hardly any are left. Many scientists fear there is no way to keep them from becoming extinct.

The kagu

Oo-ah—oo-ah—oo-ah!

A shrill, barking noise rings through the mountain forest. It sounds like the barking of a dog. But it is really the call of a bird—a bird called a kagu.

A kagu is about twenty inches long. It has gray feathers, and its legs and bill are orange-red. On its head it has a circle of long feathers that usually hang down its back. The kagu has large, powerful-looking

wings, but, strangely, it never flies. It either cannot, or will not.

Kagus live in pairs. Each pair has a part of the forest that is its very own territory. There, the two birds live and hunt. They sleep during the day, hidden in tiny caves or cracks in the rocks. At night, they hunt for worms, snails, and frogs.

At mating time, male and female kagus do a kind of dance together. The long feathers on their heads stand straight up. The birds spread their wings like capes. They strut back and forth, and move around each other in circles.

The kagus live on the island of New Caledonia, in the Pacific Ocean. About a hundred years ago, people from Europe began to hunt the kagu for its feathers. It was also hunted by dogs the Europeans brought with them. It is now against the law for people to hunt kagus, but they are still hunted by dogs. And because kagus do not fly, it is easy for the dogs to catch them.

To add to their troubles, the kagus are also losing their forest homes. The trees are being cut down for lumber. Unless something is done to help them, these strange birds that do not fly may become extinct.

The Atlantic hawksbill turtle

When a hawksbill turtle swims underwater, it looks almost like a fat bird. It holds out its big front flippers like wings, and its mouth looks like a bird's beak.

Hawksbill turtles seem to spend most of their time in shallow water, not far from land. They do not swim great distances as most other sea turtles do. They are one of the smallest of all the sea turtles. A full-grown hawksbill's shell may be about three feet long and two feet wide.

A hawksbill turtle will eat just about anything it can find in the water. It will even eat the kind of jellyfish called a Portuguese man-of-war. This animal has fearsome, stinging tentacles. But the turtle just closes its eyes to keep them from being stung.

Hawksbill turtles are in serious danger. They are hunted for their skins, their meat, and their shells. The meat makes delicious soup. The shells are made into frames for glasses. In some places, baby hawksbills are stuffed and mounted for sale to tourists. If all this killing of hawksbills goes on, these turtles will become extinct.

The dugong

All day long the two dugongs floated in deep water,
away from the land. The day is their time of rest.
But now, the sun had set. In the darkness, the big
creatures swam slowly in toward shore. It was time to
eat, and the green seaweed that is their favorite food
grows in the shallow water near shore.

The dugongs dived down into the forest of gently
waving seaweed. With their mouths, they pulled up
whole plants from the sand. They swished the plants
back and forth in the water to clean them off. Then,
without hardly chewing, they swallowed them. Every
few minutes the dugongs would swim up to the surface
for a breath of air.

Dugongs are big, slow-moving animals, often as
much as ten feet long. They live in warm seas, along
the coasts of parts of Africa, Asia, and Australia. A
dugong spends all its life in the water, but it is not a
fish. Dugongs are air breathers. They belong to the
mammal family, like dogs, cats, monkeys, and all other
air-breathing, hairy animals. However, a dugong
isn't very hairy, except around the mouth. Its skin is
hairless, tough, thick, and wrinkled. It looks like
the skin of a rhinoceros or elephant.

Dugongs are harmless and do not cause trouble for
anyone. But people hunt them for their meat and for the
oil that can be made from their fat. They already
have been wiped out in some parts of the world. In
other places, there aren't nearly as many dugongs as
there used to be.

Why Is It Happening?

Man alone, though often in
combination with his livestock,
is destroying the natural
environments of the world.

Kai Curry-Lindahl

The most dangerous enemy

The great African rhinoceros dozed in a pile of powdery dust beside an old, crumbling termite hill. It lay on its stomach, with its front legs tucked under its chest, its chin on the ground. The thick, gray skin of the black rhinoceros was as wrinkled and creased as the bark on a gnarled old tree trunk.

This was the dry season. No rain had fallen for weeks. When there were no muddy puddles to wallow in, this big dust pile was the rhino's favorite place. The big animal came here each day to doze from midmorning until late afternoon. Near sunset, it would trot off into the thickets, to browse on leaves most of the night.

Three small, brownish birds moved about on the rhino's broad back. Occasionally, the birds dug their beaks into the rhino's skin. These were oxpeckers, little birds that often stay with rhinoceroses. They feed on the insects that live on a rhino's body.

The oxpeckers had been feeling nervous for some time. Something was wrong, but they had not yet discovered what it was. From time to time they would cock their

heads and peer with bright eyes across the great yellow plain that stretched out around the termite hill. Was there a strange scent in the air? Was something out on the plain moving toward them?

There was! Suddenly they saw it. They began to screech and chatter with nervous excitement. All together, they fluttered up into the air.

The sudden commotion woke the rhino instantly. The big beast's eyes opened and it scrambled to its feet. It was not frightened. There were no animals on the great plain that could do harm to the huge, horned creature. Even a family of lions would slink out of its

way if it moved toward them. But all the rhino's
wild animal senses warned it of danger. Something was
approaching. The rhino's nearsighted eyes could see
nothing but a blur moving slowly toward it. But to its
keen nose there came a sharp, unfamiliar smell. The
rhino hesitated, as if deciding whether to lower its
head and charge, or simply turn and run away.

Crack!

A single rifle shot echoed over the plain. The rhino
fell to its knees. For nearly a minute it remained
unmoving, frozen in surprise and pain. Then, with
a great thump, it flopped over on its side and lay still.

The man with the rifle hurried to the rhino's body.
Quickly, he cut the two horns from the dead animal's
nose and stuffed them into a bag slung over his
shoulder. Then, bending low, he scurried toward a line
of scrub trees in the distance.

Panting, he knelt behind some bushes and looked
back anxiously across the plain. He was looking for a
telltale cloud of dust that would mean a car or truck
was speeding toward him. What he had just done was
against the law. If he were caught he would be put in
prison for a long time. But every rhinoceros horn he

could get was worth its weight in gold! People in many parts of Asia would pay well for just a tiny piece of rhino horn. These people believe it is a magical sort of medicine.

Satisfied that no one was coming, the man rose to his feet and set out toward his camp, which was hidden a few miles away. He had more horns there, from other rhinos he had killed. It's worth the risk, thought the man—if I can get enough horns I'll be rich! He grinned at the thought.

The rhino's big, gray body lay motionless in the dust. It was covered with a cloud of noisy, buzzing flies. Soon, vultures would come drifting down on stiff wings to squawk and squabble over the body.

The rhino had not been killed to feed hungry people. It had not been killed because it was dangerous or troublesome. It had not even been killed for sport. It had been killed because its horns are worth money. It did not matter to the man who had killed it that there are not many of these big, wonderful creatures left. He would have killed it even if he had known that it was the very last rhinoceros in the world.

Wild animals face many dangers. Other animals may hunt them for food . . . they may die from lack of food or water . . . they may be killed by forest fires, drowned in floods, or trapped in quicksand. But none of these things can destroy an entire species of animal. Only *people* can do this. People kill animals for their skins or horns. People take over animals' lands for farms, mines, and factories. People pollute the air, earth, and water with chemicals, oil, and garbage. A wild animal's most dangerous enemy is people.

Too much killing

Beneath a pale moon, shadowy shapes glided across the African plain. A frightening, chattering laugh broke the night's stillness. The hyenas were hunting!

As the hyenas moved toward a small herd of wildebeests, they scared the big, shaggy animals. The wildebeests ran for their lives. The hyenas raced after them. Quickly, they closed in on a young wildebeest that was not as fast as the others. The hyenas pulled it down, killed it, and began to feast on its flesh.

Hyenas and hawks, foxes and frogs, spiders and snakes, lions and lizards, dolphins and dragonflies—all these, and many other animals, are hunters. They hunt and kill other creatures for food. Some people think of animals that kill others as "bad," but that

hyenas catching a wildebeest

isn't true. Animals that kill others only do what they must do to stay alive.

As a matter of fact, the world *needs* hunting animals. They do a very important job. If meat-eaters, such as hyenas, did not kill some of the plant-eating animals, such as wildebeests, there would soon be too many plant-eaters. The plant-eaters would eat up all the plants in places where they live. Before long, the land would turn into a desert. Then the plant-eaters would starve. But all over the world, meat-eating animals keep other animals from increasing too much. And as long as the plant-eaters don't increase too much, the meat-eaters can't increase, either. So this kind of hunting helps keep nature in balance.

People also hunt. They hunt for sport and for food. The kind of hunting that many people do does not upset the balance of nature, either. In many countries,

(continued on page 202)

Too much killing

(continued from page 201)

people are allowed to hunt only animals that are plentiful. And they can shoot only a small number of these animals. There is no danger that all the animals will be killed off by this kind of hunting. Also, people pay money for permission to hunt. This money helps take care of places where wild animals can live.

But some kinds of hunting *do* upset the balance of nature. In many parts of the world animals are being wiped out by hunting!

Even when it is against the law to hunt some kinds of animals, there are hunters who pay no attention to the law. They hunt tigers, leopards, otters, and other animals with valuable fur. The hunters sell the skins of these animals to companies that make coats from them. Alligators are hunted for their skins, too. The skins are used to make shoes, belts, and purses. Hunters kill

elephant tusks taken by hunters

coats made of animal skins

rhinoceroses for their horns and elephants for their
tusks. There are hunters who try to kill as many of
these animals as they can, even though there are fewer
and fewer such animals. Some hunters even shoot polar
bears, eagles, and other endangered animals for "fun."

Some animals are not protected by laws. So, many
of these animals are being killed off, too. In Australia,

(continued on page 204)

Too much killing

(continued from page 203)

hunters often kill thousands of kangaroos in a single day. In North Africa, animals such as the oryx have been hunted until they are nearly all gone. And on the oceans, many kinds of whales are still hunted down by special ships and killed with harpoons fired from a kind of cannon.

Many animals are in danger of becoming extinct simply because of too much hunting. But things are now being done to protect them.

In many parts of the world, endangered animals are protected by the law. Hunters who kill these animals are punished—if they are caught. They may have to pay a fine or even go to jail. In every national park and wildlife reserve there are game wardens or rangers who can arrest hunters who break the law.

In some countries, laws have been passed to stop people from selling the meat, skin, or any other part of an endangered animal. This means that hunters who have been making money by killing lots of animals will no longer be able to sell the meat or fur of the animals they kill. If they cannot make money by killing animals, they may stop hunting them.

Laws such as these may stop much of the killing of endangered animals. Then, perhaps, the animals will be able to grow in numbers. They will no longer be in danger of becoming extinct.

There is another kind of hunting that has nearly wiped out many kinds of animals. These animals are not hunted for their skins, or meat, or horns, or tusks. They are not even hunted for "fun." They are killed

(continued on page 206)

whale being hauled onto a whaling ship

dead whales being brought
to a factory on shore

Too much killing
(continued from page 204)

off simply because some people think they are harmful or cause problems. They are "pests."

Millions of prairie dogs once lived in parts of the United States. These little animals dig tunnels in the earth, so the places where they live are filled with holes. When people began to move into these places, their cows and horses were sometimes injured when they stepped into prairie dog holes. People also thought the prairie dogs ate too much of the grass that their cattle needed.

So, to these people, prairie dogs were simply pests. The people shot, trapped, and poisoned as many prairie

skins of coyotes killed as pests

dogs as they possibly could. Now, there are not many prairie dogs left.

The same thing happened to wolves, coyotes, mountain lions, and many other kinds of animals in North America. And it happened to many animals in other parts of the world. This is why some kinds of animals are now nearly extinct.

But we are now finding out that many of these "pests" are not pests at all. Some of them are really very helpful. We have learned that prairie dogs help to make the land better for growing things. And we have found that wolves and mountain lions do an important job by controlling the numbers of plant-eating animals.

Many animal "pests" are no longer hunted and poisoned. Instead, we are trying to save them.

Changes in the land

The great, green forest stretched for miles and miles. Millions of huge trees, wrapped in thick vines, crowded together. The leaves formed a roof that shut out the sunlight and held in the heat. This made the forest hot and damp and dark.

In the upper treetops, where the sun was bright, lived the large, red-furred apes called orang-utans. The treetops were their houses, streets, and grocery stores. The orangs slept in the trees, moved through them as easily as you walk on a sidewalk, and got all their food from them.

The orangs were always on the move. As soon as
they ate the best leaves, juiciest buds, and ripest fruits
in one place, the apes moved to another place. There
was always plenty of food to be found in the enormous
forest. Even in the places where all the food had been
eaten, it would soon grow back again.

(continued on page 210)

Changes in the land

(continued from page 209)

As families of orang-utans moved about through the huge forest, they often met each other. This was how the young female and male orangs found mates and started new families.

For thousands of years the orang-utans lived this way in their forest home. There was plenty of food. They had no enemies. There was a lot of room in the great forest. So there were many thousands of orangs.

Then, men came. And they changed the face of the land. They cut down the great trees. The wood was needed to build houses. The land where the trees stood was needed for farms.

Soon the forest was much smaller. And so was the number of orang-utans. There was not enough room for all of them any more. There was not enough food to go around.

Some of the orangs were forced out of the forest, into places where they could not live. Others were left in tiny groups in small bits of forest that had not been cleared. But these small patches of forest were widely separated. The orangs living in these small areas were cut off from others of their kind. Now, many of them would never find mates and raise families.

Most wild animals can live only in places where the plants or animals they need also live. Many animals need lots of room to search for food and find mates.

(continued on page 212)

clearing a forest for farmland

Changes in the land
(continued from page 210)

If people take over and change most of the land, many kinds of animals will die out.

Another kind of danger often comes to animals when people move into their lands. The people sometimes bring other animals with them—animals from other parts of the world. This often causes serious trouble.

Little birds called Stephen Island wrens once lived on a tiny, rocky island in the Pacific Ocean. These plump birds had brownish feathers, short tails, and wings that were too small for flying. There weren't many wrens, because there wasn't much food for them on the island. But the wrens lived very well. There were no animals that hunted them, and no animals could get to the island.

But if animals couldn't get to the island, people in boats could. One day, men came. They built a lighthouse. Then the man in charge of the lighthouse came—and he brought a cat with him.

The cat soon discovered the wrens. It began to hunt them. The wrens were helpless. They had never been hunted by an enemy before. They couldn't fly and they didn't know how to hide. Before long, the cat had killed them all. The Stephen Island wren is extinct.

Every place in the world has its own kinds of animals. If other kinds of animals are brought from somewhere else, they often cause trouble. Sometimes the new animals hunt and kill many of the native animals, as the cat did. Sometimes they take over the native animals' food.

There is really only one good way to protect animals from such "outsiders." The "outsiders" must be kept away. Little reptiles called tuataras were nearly wiped out because sheep were brought to the islands where the tuataras lived. The sheep ate the grass where the tuataras hunted for food. The tuataras all died out on many of the islands.

But then, a few islands where tuataras still lived were turned into protected places. No sheep or any other "outsider" animals were permitted on the islands. This saved the tuataras.

(continued on page 215)

Changes in the land
(continued from page 213)

Turning places where wild animals live into protected places, such as the tuataras' islands, is the best way of protecting animals from all kinds of problems. Many countries have made large parts of forests, plains, and mountains into protected places. These places are called national parks or animal reserves.

In most parks and reserves, no trees can be cut down, no houses or factories can be built, no hunting is allowed, and no animals can be brought in from somewhere else. The land is kept wild, just as it has been for many thousands of years. The animals in these places are protected. They have the kind of land they need and room to live the way they must.

Here, and on the next few pages, you can see what some of these parks and reserves look like, and the kinds of animals that live in them.

(text continued on page 224)

Kootenay National Park, Canada

This park is a beautiful northern pine forest in the Canadian Rockies. Many forest and mountain animals, such as grizzly bears and bald eagles, live here. The animals in the picture are American elk, also called *wapiti.*

hippopotamus

cheetah

zebra

Changes in the land
(continued from page 215)

This African park is a great grassy plain. The park lies at the foot of snow-capped Mount Kilimanjaro. Lions, cheetahs, zebras, and wildebeests live here.

Masai Amboseli National Park, Kenya

(continued on page 219)

Changes in the land
(continued from page 217)

Ayers Rock—Mount Olga National Park, Australia

This park is in a hot, dry desert. It is the home of dingoes, wallaroos, and many other kinds of animals. The huge boulder, called Ayers Rock, is more than a thousand feet high.

emu

dingo

wedge-tailed eagle

wallaroo

(continued on page 220)

Changes in the land

(continued from page 219)

black howler monkey

macaw

Iguaçu National Park, Brazil

Howler monkeys, macaws, spectacled bears,
and giant anteaters live in this hot, damp
forest. The huge waterfall, known as Iguaçu
Falls, is more than two miles wide.

(continued on page 222)

Changes in the land

(continued from page 220)

Sambar deer, swamp deer, and other hoofed animals roam these grassy plains and woodlands. Pangolins, jungle fowl, tigers, and many other creatures are also found here.

Kanha National Park, India

pangolin

jungle fowl

sambar deer

(continued on page 224)

San Diego Wild Animal Park

Changes in the land
(continued from page 222)

It is not always possible to save places for animals in their own lands. So some animals that are in danger are moved to new homes—homes much like those where they were born. But the new homes are many thousands of miles away in other countries.

The San Diego Wild Animal Park is such a place. This animal reserve is a huge section of land in southern California. It is very much like the land in parts of Asia and Africa. Many kinds of African and Asian animals have been brought to the park to live. This park is a kind of zoo. But it is more than just a place where people can look at animals. It's a way of saving

animals. Scientists at the park study the animals to
learn more about how they live.

Some of the animals that are in the San Diego Wild
Animal Park are in danger in their own countries. But
in the park they are safe and protected. They have
some freedom and are able to live somewhat as they
did in the wild. They are not kept in cages, but are out
in the open where they have plenty of room to move
around. They are able to have babies and increase their
numbers. This doesn't always happen when animals
are kept in cages in ordinary zoos.

Other places like the San Diego Wild Animal Park
are being built. Even though certain kinds of wild
animals may become extinct in their own lands, some
will be safe and sound in new homes in other lands.

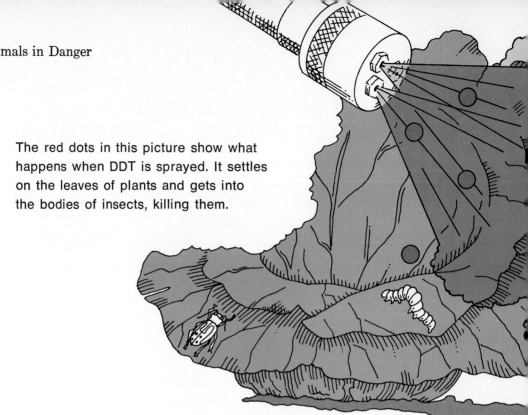

The red dots in this picture show what happens when DDT is sprayed. It settles on the leaves of plants and gets into the bodies of insects, killing them.

Poisoned earth, water, and air

Mr. Jones was worried. He had found some big green caterpillars munching on two of the cabbages in his garden. If he didn't protect his plants, insects might destroy them all.

So Mr. Jones bought some cans of stuff called pesticide. This is a poison that kills insects. Mr. Jones sprayed the pesticide over his garden several times a week. Many of his neighbors used pesticide on their bushes and plants, too.

The pesticide seemed to work well. A cabbage moth fluttered down to lay her eggs on one of Mr. Jones's cabbages. The moth quickly died. A bean beetle tried to make a meal of one of Mr. Jones's bean plants. It, too, was quickly killed by the poison. But so were a lot of harmless insects—insects that could have been used as food by the birds.

Each time it rained, a lot of the pesticide washed off the plants and soaked into the ground where earthworms lived. As the worms crawled about on their earthworm business, eating their way through the soil, the pesticide got into their bodies. It didn't kill them, but they soon had a lot of it in their bodies.

One morning, a bright-breasted robin spied a worm in Mr. Jones's yard. The worm quickly became the robin's breakfast. Next morning, the robin was back again to catch another worm. This was a good place to hunt, so the robin began to come every day. Other robins came, too.

(continued on page 228)

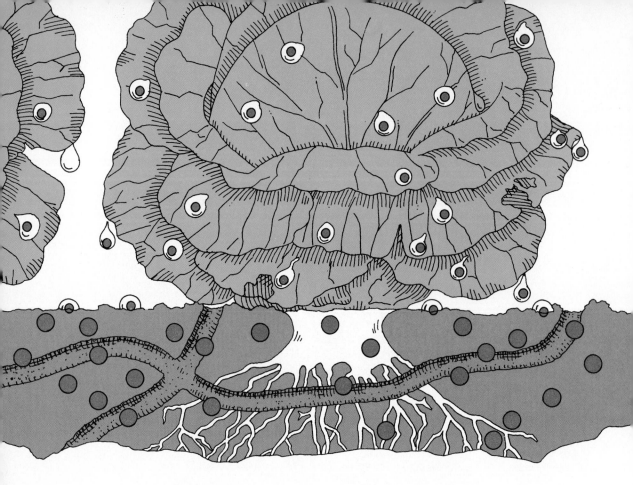

Poisoned earth, water, and air
(continued from page 227)

One day when Mr. Jones came out to weed his garden, he found two dead robins lying in the grass. Sadly, he dug a small hole and buried the birds. He wondered what had killed them.

The robins had been poisoned. They had been poisoned by the pesticide Mr. Jones and his neighbors had sprayed. The worms in the ground were filled with pesticide. When the robins ate the worms, the pesticide went into the robins' bodies. After a while there was so much pesticide in the robins that it killed them.

There was trouble in other places, too. Gardeners and farmers for miles around had sprayed their gardens and crops with pesticide. Rain washed a lot of the pesticide into nearby streams that flowed into a small

Much of the DDT soaks into the ground. It gets into the bodies of earthworms. Robins and other small birds that eat the worms get DDT in their bodies. Too much can kill them.

lake. Soon there was a lot of pesticide in the lake. The bodies of the fish and other creatures that lived in the lake were filled with this poison.

A flock of large birds called ospreys lived near the lake. They swooped over the water, catching fish that swam near the top. The more fish the ospreys ate, the more pesticide got into their bodies.

The pesticide did not kill the ospreys. But it did cause changes inside their bodies. When it came time for the female ospreys to lay eggs, the changes in their bodies made them lay eggs with shells so thin they would nearly all break, killing the babies inside. Instead of a dozen or so new little ospreys to help the flock grow, there were only a few.

The pesticide that caused all this trouble is called DDT. For many years, farmers all over the world used DDT to protect their crops from hungry insects. It was

(continued on page 231)

DDT also gets into streams, lakes, and ponds. It goes into the bodies of fish. Ospreys and other birds eat the fish and the DDT goes into their bodies.

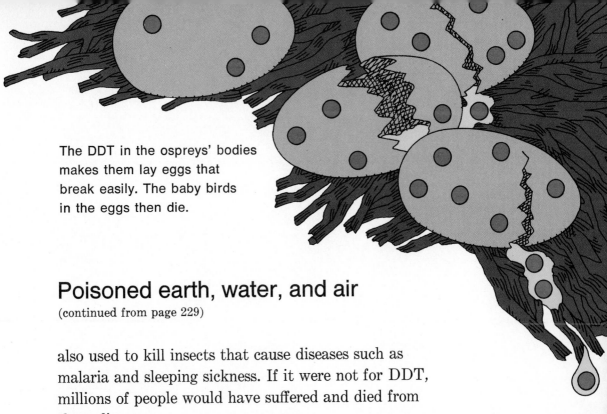

The DDT in the ospreys' bodies makes them lay eggs that break easily. The baby birds in the eggs then die.

Poisoned earth, water, and air

(continued from page 229)

also used to kill insects that cause diseases such as malaria and sleeping sickness. If it were not for DDT, millions of people would have suffered and died from these diseases.

A lot of DDT was used. It soaked into the earth and water everywhere in the world. And it is still there. There is no way to get rid of it. It is still killing some animals and poisoning others, especially fish-eating birds such as ospreys and eagles.

People in most parts of the world have stopped using DDT. But where DDT is still in the earth and water, it will cause trouble for a long time to come. Many new pesticides are now being used, but some of these are just as harmful to wildlife as DDT. Some pesticides must be used, so scientists are trying to find kinds that work well, but do not harm wildlife.

Pesticides are only one kind of pollution that causes trouble for animals. There are other kinds of pollution that cause trouble, too.

Chimneys and car engines fill the air with smoke. This smoke is made of different kinds of gases mixed with millions of tiny bits of rock and metal. Most of these gases are poisonous. This dirty air can make animals, plants, and people sick. It can even kill them.

(continued on page 232)

Poisoned earth, water, and air

(continued from page 231)

Lakes and rivers are polluted by sewage from towns and cities. An even worse kind of water pollution comes from factories that dump used-up chemicals into lakes and rivers. Many of these chemicals are poisons. The water soon becomes so bad animals cannot drink it. Creatures that live in the water are killed by the poisons.

smoke-polluted air and oil-polluted water

Big, ocean-going ships called tankers carry oil
from one place to another. But these tankers are one-way
cargo ships. They can't be sailed back empty. To
make them safe for the return voyage, seawater is
pumped into the oil tanks. Later, this dirty water is
pumped out. If this is done at sea, great oil slicks form
on the surface of the ocean. Many kinds of fish and
other water creatures have been poisoned or killed by
these giant oil slicks.

(continued on page 235)

Poisoned earth, water, and air

(continued from page 233)

Sometimes the oily sludge is pumped out near the shore, or floats in toward the shore. Then the oil slick is a threat to sea birds. Auks, gulls, cormorants, ducks, and other fish-eating birds dive into the water to get their food. When they dive into an oil slick, the oil covers their feathers. Then the birds can no longer swim or fly. They are faced with a slow death. Hundreds of thousands of sea birds have been killed in this way.

If pollution is such a dreadful problem, what are we doing about it?

More and more factories have machinery to clean up the smoke that comes from furnaces. Many countries are working to clean up polluted rivers and lakes. We are putting special equipment on cars and trucks to clean up the gases they pour into the air. Companies that own fleets of oil tankers have agreed not to let their ships dump oily water into the sea.

Pollution is still a threat to wild animals, plants, and people. But we are trying to reduce and control it.

students testing water for pollution

Helping Animals in Danger

Those who wish to pet and baby wild animals "love" them. But those who respect their natures and wish to let them live normal lives love them more.

Edwin Way Teale

A helping hand for whoopers

The small group of men stood on the muddy shore of a shallow lagoon. With anxious eyes, they looked into the sky.

Suddenly, one of the men pointed. "Here they come!" The men could just make out two black dots moving toward them—still high in the sky and far away. As the shapes came closer, the men could see two large, white birds clearly. Flying through the air with steadily beating wings, they were as swift and graceful as ballet dancers. Then, with their great, black-tipped wings stiffly outstretched, the birds skimmed down to land easily in the shallow water.

The first members of the whooping crane flock had returned to their winter home. They were back at the Aransas Refuge on the coast of Texas.

The men continued to watch the sky. Would all the cranes who had left in the spring come safely back? Had any new ones hatched during the summer?

"Here come two more. They have a young one!"

During the next few weeks, more cranes continued to arrive. Finally, they were all back. This time there were forty-eight of them—the only flock of wild whooping cranes in the world.

Once, there had been several thousand cranes and several flocks. They went flapping northward each spring and came soaring back south each fall. The birds spent their summers on the lakes and ponds of Canada, Minnesota, North Dakota, Iowa, and Illinois. They mated and built nests among the cattails. They laid eggs and raised their babies.

In the autumn, when leaves became tinted with gold and flame, the cranes and their young ones returned to the swamps and marshes of Florida, Texas, and Louisiana. This had been their way of life for half a million years.

But there came a time when the land began to change. People came in greater and greater numbers. They built houses and turned vast sections of wild prairie into farmland. Towns sprang up on the shores of lakes where cranes built their nests. Soon, there was not enough room for the cranes.

There were also new enemies—hunters with guns and people who collected birds' eggs for fun. Hundreds of cranes were shot as they waded in lakes, sat on their nests, or winged through the sky. Hundreds of eggs were taken from nests, never to hatch.

Year by year, there were fewer and fewer whooping cranes. By the 1890's they were seldom seen in the places they once had lived. Most of those that were left were hidden in wild places where people hadn't yet hunted them or searched for their nests. But men still shot them whenever they were seen. People still robbed their nests whenever any were found.

Within a few years, there were no whooping cranes to be seen anywhere. Most scientists were sure they had become extinct.

But in 1936, a scientist named Neil Hotchkiss discovered that the cranes were not extinct. He found four of them. They were living on a small bit of marshland on the Texas coast.

Other scientists became interested. They found that there were eighteen whooping cranes living in the marshland. It was the last winter home for the last flock of whooping cranes in the world.

Many people soon offered to help save the birds. The United States government bought the bit of land and turned it into a protected place where the birds would

be safe. It became known as the Aransas National Wildlife Refuge. Scientists were put in charge of it, to study the whooping cranes and help protect them.

It wasn't an easy job. The refuge was not as safe a place as people thought. Even though everyone knew how rare the birds were, hunters sometimes tried to sneak into the refuge to shoot them!

But with the help of the people who work at the refuge, the whooping crane flock has survived. For a number of years, the flocks even got larger. In

1950, there were thirty-one birds. In 1960, there were thirty-six. In 1970, there were fifty-seven.

But sometimes the flock gets smaller. In 1973, there were only forty-eight of the birds. So the whooping cranes are still in danger. Something could easily happen to wipe them all out.

However, the whooping crane *has* been saved, for a while at least. Something *is* being done to protect it. And this shows that maybe something *can* be done for all the world's vanishing animals.

Chimpanzee friends

Pooch—Olly—Goblin—David Graybeard—and old
Mr. Worzle. These are some of the names that Jane
van Lawick-Goodall gave to her wild chimpanzee
friends.

Jane Goodall is a scientist. For several years she
lived with wild chimpanzees in a forest in Africa.
For the first six months, the chimps ran away whenever
they saw her. But slowly they grew used to her. In
time, some of them even became friendly.

She found that the chimps sometimes hunt and kill
other animals for food. She saw that they often make
very simple tools. And she found that each chimpanzee
is different from every other chimpanzee—just as
people are different from each other.

Jane Goodall wrote two books about her friends,
the wild chimpanzees. She described how these smart
animals are being hunted and pushed out of the places
where they live. She said that this is a terrible
thing, because we can learn much about ourselves by
studying chimpanzees. But to do this, we need to
study the chimps where they live—not in zoos.

Many scientists are interested in the work Jane
Goodall is doing with chimpanzees. Other people who
are interested in saving these animals are collecting
money to start special parks in Africa. Here
chimpanzees can be protected from people. They can
live as they have always lived.

Gerald Durrell and a thick-billed parrot

A very special zoo

A bird called a white-eared pheasant once lived in parts of China and Tibet. But no white-eared pheasants had been seen in these countries for a long time. Most scientists thought they might be extinct.

Then, a few years ago, a zoo on the island of Jersey, between England and France, got hold of four white-eared pheasants from a dealer in animals. This zoo is a very special kind of zoo. The people here try to save animals from becoming extinct. They collect animals that are in danger. They try to get them to have babies that can be reared and cared for in the zoo. This is not easy, because some animals do not seem able to have babies when they live in a zoo.

But one of the white-eared pheasants laid six eggs. The people who work at the zoo helped to hatch the eggs and rear the baby chicks. When the chicks were grown, they began to lay eggs, too. By 1973, there were more than fifty white-eared pheasants!

So the white-eared pheasant may have been saved. Many other kinds of animals that are in danger of becoming extinct have also been reared at this zoo— more than a thousand of them!

The zoo is the Jersey Wildlife Preservation Trust. It is owned by Gerald Durrell. Ever since he was a little boy, Mr. Durrell has loved animals. He has always dreamed of having his very own zoo. His dream came true. Today he does have a zoo of his own—a zoo that helps to save animals that are in danger.

Elsa and Pippa

What would you do if someone brought you three
tiny, helpless lion cubs whose mother was dead?

That's what happened to Joy Adamson. Her husband
was a game warden in Africa. One day he brought
home three orphaned lion cubs. Two of the cubs were
sent to a zoo, but Mrs. Adamson couldn't bear to
part with the smallest cub. She kept it.

cheetahs

The cub grew into a big, beautiful, healthy lioness that acted like a big, pet house cat. Mrs. Adamson named the lioness Elsa. She wrote the story of Elsa in a famous book, *Born Free*. Elsa's story was also made into an exciting motion picture.

That was many years ago. But ever since, Joy Adamson has been interested in helping animals. She is particularly worried about cheetahs, which are in danger of becoming extinct. She raised a cheetah, just as she did Elsa, and wrote books about the cheetah, too. These books are *Pippa: The Cheetah and Her Cubs*, and *Pippa's Challenge*.

Mrs. Adamson used the money she made from the books and movies to start Elsa Clubs around the world. These clubs work to protect endangered animals, such as the cheetah.

Saving the ospreys

Ospreys are big, brown and white birds that catch fish. And they are in great danger from a chemical called DDT. Farmers used to use DDT to kill insects that ruin crops. Much of this DDT got into lakes and rivers. The DDT poisoned the fish in the lakes and rivers. When ospreys caught and ate the fish, the DDT poisoned the ospreys, too.

Ospreys poisoned by DDT lay eggs with shells that are too thin. The eggs break easily. If this happens, the baby chicks die before they can hatch. Each year, fewer and fewer osprey chicks are hatched. So ospreys are slowly becoming fewer each year.

But two young scientists may have found a way to save the ospreys. One of them, Robert Kennedy, found that if an osprey's eggs are taken from its nest, the female will often lay more eggs. The other scientist, Paul Spitzer, discovered that an osprey will hatch another osprey's eggs if they are put into its nest.

These men take healthy eggs that some ospreys have laid and put them into the nests of ospreys that can't lay healthy eggs. The birds hatch the healthy eggs and raise the chicks. And the birds whose eggs were stolen lay more eggs and hatch chicks from them. So the two scientists are helping the ospreys to have more babies.

It is now against the law in many countries to use sprays with DDT in them, so perhaps the trouble will stop. The pollution isn't all gone, but if the ospreys can keep having enough babies, these beautiful birds may be saved.

an osprey feeding its young

Paul Spitzer collecting osprey eggs

The gorillas next door

Dr. George Schaller is a scientist who once had gorillas for neighbors!

For nearly two years, Dr. Schaller lived in a mountain forest in Africa where bands of gorillas roam. Each day, Dr. Schaller studied the gorillas as they moved about in search of food. He watched as they napped and played. Many of the gorillas grew quite used to him. Once, one of the big, shaggy animals climbed up into the tree where Dr. Schaller was sitting and sat down near him!

Dr. Schaller was one of the first men to study how gorillas live in the wild. He learned many things that hadn't been known before—such as how gorillas act toward each other, and the many different kinds of plant foods they eat. What he learned may help us to keep gorillas from becoming extinct.

A school for orphan birds

Wild eagles, hawks, and other hunting birds teach their young how to hunt. A young bird will die if it loses its parents before it has learned how to hunt for food. And this often happens. Many hunting birds are shot, even though this is against the law. Then the young birds are left helpless.

In California, people try to help orphan hunting birds. Rangers and scientists who find the orphans take them to the San Francisco Zoo. There, the young birds go to school to learn how to hunt!

Specially trained men and women take over for the birds' parents. These people teach the young birds how to catch small animals. When the birds have learned their lessons they are taken back into the wild and set free. Now they will be able to take care of themselves. They have been given a chance to live.

training a young bald eagle to hunt

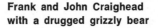
Frank and John Craighead with a drugged grizzly bear

Keeping track of grizzlies

A big, brown-furred grizzly bear plods through a thick forest on a mountainside in Yellowstone National Park in the Western United States. Around its neck, the bear wears a collar with a small radio in it. The radio sends out a beeping noise. The bear can't hear the beeps, but men with another special radio can.

The collar was put on the bear by Frank and John Craighead. These two scientists have been studying grizzly bears for several years. With the special radio and other equipment, the Craigheads keep track of every bear wearing a collar. They find out how far

it travels each day in search of food. They know
how long it stays in one place. They discover where
it builds its winter den.

The radio collar is only one of many ways the
Craighead brothers find out about grizzly bears. The
two scientists worry about grizzlies, because the big
bears seem to be dying out. There are now only about
two hundred grizzlies in the park. Each year, more
bears die than are born. The Craigheads hope to find
ways of keeping these animals from becoming extinct.

How do the Craigheads get the collars onto the
bears? They catch the bears in special traps that don't
hurt them. Then they put the bears to sleep with
drugs. While the bears sleep—on go the collars.

What you can do

There are many things you, your friends, and your family can do to help all kinds of animals.

Around the house

If you can, put a birdhouse or bird feeder in your yard.

Don't use weedkillers or other garden sprays that contain DDT or other poisons that may pollute the earth and nearby ponds. Such sprays can kill many useful insects and can poison worms and fish. They can even cause the death of birds and other small animals.

Camping, fishing, hunting, or picnicking

You can help animals most just by leaving them alone! Don't capture such small creatures as garter snakes, frogs, toads, and turtles for pets. Leave them in the wild, where they can live, and have babies, and do their part to keep nature in balance.

Don't kill animals such as snakes and spiders just because you don't like them or because you fear them. Most of these animals are harmless to people. They also play an important part in keeping things in balance.

Obey the hunting and fishing laws. Don't overhunt or overfish—many animals are in trouble because of this. Don't shoot animals that you aren't supposed to.

(continued on page 260)

What you can do
(continued from page 259)

Vacationing

Don't take animals of any kind, or anything that might have insect eggs in it, from one part of the world to another. This often causes serious trouble to plant and animal life.

When you get a pet

Don't make a pet of an animal such as a monkey, lizard, or other creature that needs special living conditions or that may grow quite large. In the past, many people bought baby alligators as pets. Then they had to get rid of them when they began to get big. This is one reason alligators are in trouble now.

Animals We Have Saved

No civilization is complete which does not include the dumb and defenseless of God's creatures within the sphere of charity and mercy.

Queen Victoria

The last-minute rescue

It was nearly dawn. The great, grassy prairie was still almost hidden in night's blackness. All was silent, except for the hum of insects.

A man crouched behind a clump of sagebrush, a rifle in his hands. At his side lay a cartridge belt filled with bullets. Three hundred yards in front of him, he could just make out some big, shaggy shapes huddled together. They were buffalo—part of the huge herd that moved across the prairie each day, feeding on the thick grass.

Slowly, the eastern edge of the sky turned pink as the sun began to rise. Dawn filled the prairie with pale gray light. The buffalo stood, ready to follow their leader, an old female. But as the light grew stronger, the man soon spotted the leader. Raising his rifle, he took careful aim at her.

The old female staggered with shock and pain when the bullet thudded into her back. She sank into a

crouch, unable to move. The sound of the shot was too far away to disturb the other buffalo. The hunter knew they would not move without their leader. Now he could pick them off one at a time.

He aimed at another, and fired. As the big creature crumpled to the ground, the other buffalo were not frightened, only confused. They milled about, but did not run away. The hunter took his time. After each shot he waited for the animals to calm down. Then he fired again. He was an expert shot. Each bullet he fired killed a buffalo almost instantly.

The hunter wiped out the entire band in little more

than half an hour. Twenty shaggy bodies lay unmoving on the plain. Now the hunter would get his helpers, men called skinners, to cut away the brown, furry hides of the dead buffalo. The hides would be packed with the hundreds of hides from other buffalo the hunter had already killed. These would be sold to companies that used them to make leather products.

This was in the year 1872. Buffalo were being killed this way all over the Western plains. There were thousands of hunters. Each killed twenty, thirty, or forty buffalo a day. In the next three years, more than six million of these big animals were killed.

The killing went on and on. Most people did not know that it was happening. Many of those who did, did not care. Some even wanted the buffalo wiped out to "make way for progress." At one time, about sixty million buffalo had roamed the plains. But by 1889, less than six hundred were left.

People suddenly began to wake up to the fact that the buffalo—the American bison—was nearly extinct. A group of scientists who went west to collect some buffalo skins for a museum were shocked—they hunted for three months, but could not find a single buffalo. Most of the men who had made their living hunting buffalo had to find new work.

A few people owned small herds of buffalo that they kept on ranches. Some of these animals were bought by the United States government and put into Yellowstone National Park, where they could be protected. But they were not protected well enough— hunters even went into the park to shoot buffalo. In the year 1893, it was found that 116 of the park buffalo had been killed. Only twenty were left.

Suddenly, many people became angry. A law against killing buffalo was quickly passed. More buffalo were bought from ranches and put into the park. Workers were hired to protect them. Money was raised to buy

more buffalo, and to buy land for a new National
Bison Range. In Canada, too, land was put aside, and
buffalo were bought to start new herds.

And so, almost at the last minute, the buffalo was
rescued. The tiny herds were protected and cared for.
They grew. Today, there are more than twenty
thousand buffalo in North America. The largest single
herd lives in the huge Wood Buffalo National Park
in Canada. There will never be as many buffalo as there
were before. But it is good to know that some of these
great, shaggy brown beasts still roam the prairie. We
did not let them perish from the earth.

The egret

The birds called egrets almost became extinct. But they were saved—by a queen!

An egret is about three feet long. It has a white body, a yellow bill, and black legs and feet. About a hundred years ago, these birds lived in swamps and near lakes and rivers in many parts of North America.

Each year at nest-building time egrets grow long, beautiful feathers on their backs. In the 1890's it was the fashion to decorate women's hats with these long feathers. So the birds were killed for their feathers. Hunters usually killed the birds in their nests, while they were hatching eggs or taking care of their young. Then, of course, the eggs never hatched, or the babies died because there was no one to take care of them.

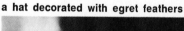

a hat decorated with egret feathers

Egrets were killed by the thousands. Some hunters even went to places where egrets were protected. Once, they murdered a game warden who was guarding a flock of egrets.

So many egrets were killed, and so many baby egrets died, that by 1908 the birds were nearly extinct. But they were saved—by the queen of England.

The queen had learned that the egrets were nearly all gone. She announced that she did not want the ladies of her court to wear hats with egret feathers on them. Most English ladies quickly stopped wearing such hats. Soon, women everywhere stopped wearing hats with egret feathers.

When hunters could no longer get money for egret feathers, they stopped killing the birds. The egrets in the United States are now protected by law, and the flocks are growing.

an egret on its nest

an old advertisement for hats made of beaver fur

The beaver

A beaver always seems to be hard at work cutting, carrying, or building. That's why when we see someone working hard we say he or she is "busy as a beaver."

This sturdy animal is about two and one-half feet long. It has brown fur and a flat, leathery tail that looks like a paddle. Its strong, sharp teeth are like chisels.

Beavers are expert builders. They use their teeth to cut down small trees and trim off the branches neatly. They eat the bark and use the logs and branches to build dams in streams. The dams hold back the water to make quiet ponds. In the ponds, the beavers build dome-shaped houses of logs, branches, and rocks, plastered with mud. We call these houses lodges.

a mother beaver feeding her young

It is hard to think of a northern forest without these skillful creatures busily at work. But for more than two hundred years the beaver was the most hunted animal in North America. For a long time, men in Europe and America wore felt hats and vests made from beaver fur. More than a hundred thousand beavers were killed every year—just for their fur. By the year 1900, not many beavers were left.

But the beavers were lucky. They were saved—not because people *tried* to save them, but because beaver-fur hats and vests went out of style. Beaver fur was no longer worth a lot of money, so beavers were no longer hunted.

Slowly, the number of beavers began to increase. Today there are many of them in the forests and streams of North America. Once again, busy beavers are at work building their dams and lodges.

The tuatara

Imagine a lizard and a bird living together in a hole in the ground! That sounds like something from a fairy tale—but it's true. On some tiny islands in the Pacific Ocean there are little reptiles called tuataras. The tuataras live in burrows that they share with birds called mutton birds!

Tuataras are about two feet long. They eat beetles, worms, snails, grasshoppers, and other insects. Tuataras look like lizards, but they are not lizards. They are the last living members of a family of reptiles that has lived on the earth for more than 200 million years. There were tuataras long before there were snakes, lizards, crocodiles, or even dinosaurs!

It would have been sad if tuataras had become extinct after such a long time. But this nearly happened.

Tuataras once lived on the big island of New Zealand, as well as on many small islands nearby. Then people came with their dogs and pigs. These animals easily caught and ate the slow-moving tuataras. Later, sheep were brought to the islands. The sheep ate the grass in which the tuataras hunted for insects. This drove away most of the insects, so there was no longer enough food for the tuataras.

The tuataras on New Zealand and most of the larger islands were all wiped out. But some were left on a few of the small islands. The government of New Zealand made the small islands protected places. People may not visit these islands.

This saved the tuataras. There are now about ten thousand of these little reptiles. They live on their lonely little islands in much the same way their ancestors did millions of years ago.

The trumpeter swan

The trumpeter swan gets its name from the sound it makes—a sound like the note of a trumpet. The biggest kind of swan in North America, this beautiful creature is about five feet long.

Trumpeter swans were once a common sight on lakes and ponds in many parts of North America. Great flocks of them formed big V's in the sky when they flew north in the spring and south in the fall. But wherever the swans came down to build their nests and stay for a while, they were hunted for their feathers and meat. Each year, fewer and fewer were seen.

Finally, a law against hunting the swans was passed. But many people feared the law was too late. In 1932 there were only fifty-seven trumpeter swans left. Most scientists thought the swans would surely become extinct.

Then, in 1935, one of the places where trumpeter swans still lived and built nests was made into a refuge—a protected place. Left alone, with no people to bother them or hunt them, the swans began to increase. Today, there are about five thousand of them. They are out of danger.

some toy bears were once covered with koala fur

The koala

The Australian "teddy bear," the little koala, was nearly killed off because of its warm, gray fur.

Koalas are harmless little animals, about two feet long. They eat only the leaves and buds of the eucalyptus tree, so they spend most of their lives in these trees. A koala climbs down to the ground only when it wants to move to another tree.

a koala eating eucalyptus leaves

Because they are slow-moving and easy to find, koalas are easy to hunt. For many years, millions of the little creatures were killed. After a time, very few were left anywhere in Australia.

But many Australians, as well as people in other countries, wanted to save the koalas. President Herbert Hoover stopped koala skins from being brought into the United States. The governments of Australian states passed laws to stop the hunting of koalas. These lovable little animals were saved.

Père David's deer

If it weren't for an English duke, the little deer called Père David's deer would be extinct today. They were saved by the Duke of Bedford.

Père David's deer have longer tails than other kinds of deer, and very broad hoofs. They are not quite four feet high. Long ago, there were many of these deer in China, where they were called *mi-lu*. But lands where they roamed were taken over by people. The deer began to disappear. Some of the places where herds of the deer still lived became parks. The deer in these parks became used to people, and grew quite tame. After a while, there were no wild *mi-lu* left—only tame ones in parks.

And after a long while, there was only one herd left. It was kept in a great park that belonged to the Chinese emperors. Few people got to see these deer. People who lived in other countries did not even know of them.

In 1865, a French priest, Père (Father) Armand David, was traveling in China. He saw the deer and told scientists in Europe about them. A few of the deer were bought by European zoos. Because Père David had discovered them, they were named after him.

Years later, trouble came to the part of China where the deer lived. There were floods, and people were starving. The water broke down the wall of the park and most of the deer escaped. They were killed and eaten by starving people. The rest of the deer were later killed, too. By 1921 there were no longer any Père David's deer in China. The only ones left were a few in zoos in Europe.

The Duke of Bedford heard of this. He realized that the Père David's deer in the zoos would soon grow old

and die. Then this rare animal would be extinct—gone forever. So the duke bought as many deer as he could from several zoos. With these deer—sixteen of them— he started a herd. He kept the herd in a park he owned.

Today, there are more than four hundred of these deer. Many of them have been sent to zoos in all parts of the world. Some have even been sent back to their real home in China—thanks to the interest and efforts of one man, the Duke of Bedford.

The wisent

The story of the big, shaggy European bison called a wisent is much like that of Père David's deer. The wisent, too, was nearly wiped out by hungry people. And it, too, was saved because a few were in zoos.

The wisent looks much like the American bison or buffalo. But the wisent is bigger—about six feet high—and has longer legs and a smaller head. It is not an animal of the plains, like the American bison. It lives in forests. Many hundreds of years ago, big herds of wisents lived in forests in most of Europe.

But, slowly, the forests were cut down. Fewer and fewer wisents were seen. By 1900 there were only about seven hundred wild wisents. They were all in one herd in a big forest in Poland. The only other wisents were in zoos.

World War I began in 1914. Much of the fighting took place in Poland. Food ran short, especially for the armies. When hungry soldiers found a wisent, they shot it for food. By the time the fighting and trouble had ended, all the wild wisents in the forest had been killed.

But, luckily, there were still wisents in some zoos. Five of these were brought together in Poland to start a new herd. This herd was kept in captivity for more than thirty years, so there still were no wild wisents anywhere in the world. But in 1952, sixteen of the tame wisents were turned loose in the forest. Now there are more than two hundred wisents, living wild in the forest just as their ancestors did. There are also several large herds of tame wisents kept in other places. The wisent was saved.

zebras, impalas, and a wildebeest
gather at an African water hole

There is hope

The wisent, the beaver, the trumpeter swan, and a
number of other kinds of animals were once in serious
trouble. At times there were only a few of some of
these animals left, and they very nearly became
extinct. But they were saved. They are still with us
in the world.

The fact that all these animals were saved can give us hope for many of the animals that are in danger today. We know that it is possible to save many of the creatures that now face extinction, just as the wisent, the beaver, and others were saved. We can hope that all the kinds of animals that now prowl the forests, roam the plains, and gather at the water holes will still be with us in the world tomorrow—and for all the days to come.

Endangered Animals

This is a list of more than four hundred of the animals that most scientists think are in danger of becoming extinct. The animal names printed in heavy black letters are animals talked about in this book. This is only a partial list. A list of *all* the endangered animals, including fish and insects, would have more than a thousand names!

The antelope skull is the symbol for animals that are in danger. The symbol is used by the American Association of Zoological Parks and Aquariums. When you see this symbol near the cage of an animal at a zoo, you will know that kind of animal is in danger of becoming extinct.

Endangered Mammals

addax
African cheetah
African wild dog
Amazonian manatee
Arabian dorcas gazelle
Arabian gazelle
Arabian oryx
Arabian tahr
Asiatic cheetah
Asiatic lion
Asiatic wild dog
Assam rabbit
Atlantic walrus
aye-aye
bald uakari
Baluchistan bear
banded hare-wallaby
Barbary hyena
Barbary leopard
barren-ground grizzly bear
beach meadow vole
Bengal tiger
big-eared kangaroo rat

black lemur
black-footed ferret
black-headed uakari
black rhinoceros
black-tailed prairie dog
Block Island meadow vole
blue whale
Brazilian three-banded armadillo
brown hyena
Cameroon clawless otter
Caribbean monk seal
Caspian tiger
Ceylon elephant
chimpanzee
chinchilla (wild)
Chinese tiger
Columbia white-tailed deer
common dolphin
Corsican deer
crescent nail-tailed wallaby
Cuban solenodon
Delmarva Peninsula fox squirrel
desert rat kangaroo

Endangered Mammals (continued)

Dominican hutia
dorcas gazelle
douc langur
dugong
eastern jerboa marsupial
fat-tailed dwarf lemur
fin whale
Florida cougar
Florida manatee
Formosan clouded leopard
Formosan sika
fossa
Ganges River dolphin
gaur
giant anteater
giant armadillo
giant otter
glacier bear
golden-headed tamarin
golden lion marmoset
golden-rumped tamarin
gray gentle lemur
gray kangaroo
hairy-nosed wombat
Hartman's mountain zebra
humpback whale
Indiana bat
Indian rhinoceros
Indian wild ass
indri
jaguar
Javan rhinoceros
Javan tiger
Jentink's duiker
Kabal markhor
Kaibab squirrel
Kashmir stag
kit fox
kouprey
La Plata otter
leopard
Lesueur's rat kangaroo

lowland anoa
lowland gorilla
Malabar civet
Malagasy civet
Malayan tapir
maned wolf
marsh deer
Mediterranean monk seal
Mexican grizzly bear
Mexican prairie dog
mongoose lemur
mountain anoa
mountain gorilla
mountain tapir
Mhorr gazelle
North American grizzly bear
North China sika
northern Simian fox
ocelot
orang-utan
Pacific walrus
Pelzeln's gazelle
pig-footed bandicoot
pig-tailed langur
polar bear
Przewalski's horse
pygmy chimpanzee
pygmy hippopotamus
Pyrenean desman
Pyrenean ibex
rabbit-eared bandicoot
red-fronted lemur
red kangaroo
red lechwe
red-tailed sportive lemur
red uakari
red wolf
ring-tailed rock wallaby
Rio de Oro gazelle
rufous rat kangaroo
rusty numbat
Ryukyu spiny rat

(continued on next page)

Endangered Mammals (continued)

saiga antelope
Saimaa seal
sand gazelle
Sanford's lemur
scaly tailed possum
scimitar-horned oryx
Sclater's lemur
Shansi sika
shapu
Shortridge's mouse
siamang
Siberian tiger
Sikkim stag
Sinai leopard
slender-horned gazelle
small-eared dog
smoky mouse
snow leopard
snub-nosed langur
Sonoran pronghorn
South Andean huemal
South China sika
southern river otter
southern sea otter
Spanish lynx
spectacled bear
spotted bat

straight-horned markhor
Sumatran rhinoceros
Sumatran short-eared rabbit
Sumatran serow
swamp deer
Swayne's hartebeest
Tana River red colobus
Tana River mangabey
Tasmanian wolf
Texas kangaroo rat
Texas ocelot
Thailand brow-antlered deer
timber wolf
Utah prairie dog
vicuña
volcano rabbit
walia ibex
West African manatee
western giant eland
western hare-wallaby
western woolly avahi
white (square-lipped) rhinoceros
wild Bactrian camel
wild yak
Wilson's palm squirrel
woolly spider monkey
yellow-cheeked vole

Endangered Birds

African lammergeyer
Alaotra grebe
Aldabra kestrel
Andes eared grebe
Anjouan Island sparrow hawk
Anjouan scops owl
Antipodes Island parakeet
ashy ground thrush
Attwater's prairie chicken
Aukland Island rail
Australian night parrot

Bachman's warbler
Bahamas parrot
bald eagle
black-necked crane
Blyth's tragopan
brown-eared pheasant
Cabot's tragopan
California condor
Charles Island mockingbird
Chatham Island pigeon
Chatham Island robin

Endangered Birds (continued)

cheer pheasant
Chinese egret
Chinese monal
Christmas Island goshawk
cloven feathered dove
Cocos Island flycatcher
Cocos mangrove cuckoo
Colombian red-eyed cowbird
crested honeycreeper
Cuban hook-billed kite
Cuban ivory-billed woodpecker
Cuban sandhill crane
Cuban sharp-shinned hawk
dark-rumped petrel
Edward's pheasant
Elliot's pheasant
Eskimo curlew
Euler's flycatcher
Everglade kite
Florida sandhill crane
Forbes' parakeet
Galapagos hawk
Galapagos penguin
giant ibis
giant imperial pigeon
giant scops owl
golden-shouldered paradise parakeet
Grand Cayman troupial
gray-necked rock-fowl
great Indian bustard
greater prairie chicken
Grenada dove
Hawaiian crow
Hawaiian duck
Hawaiian gallinule
Hawaiian hawk
Hawaiian stilt
helmeted honeyeater
hooded crane
hooded paradise parrot
horned guan
horned parakeet

imperial parrot
imperial pheasant
imperial woodpecker
ivory-billed woodpecker
Jamaica black rail
Japanese ancient murrelet
Japanese crane
Japanese crested ibis
kagu
kakapo
Kauai alauwahio
Kauai oo
Kauai thrush
Koch's pitta
Lake Junin grebe
Laysan duck
Laysan finch-bill
long-tailed ground roller
long-toed pigeon
Madagascar teal
Malaysian peacock pheasant
maleo
Marianas pegapode
Marquesas ground dove
Martinique brown trembler
Martinique white-breasted thrasher
masked bobwhite
masked parakeet
Maui nukupuu
Maui parrotbill
Mauritius cuckoo shrike
Mauritius kestrel
Mauritius pink pigeon
Mauritius ring-necked parakeet
Mexican duck
Mikado pheasant
Mindoro imperial pigeon
Moheli green pigeon
Molokai thrush
monkey-eating eagle
Nauru nightingale warbler
New Zealand brown teal

(continued on next page)

New Zealand laughing owl
New Zealand shore plover
Nihoa finch-bill
Nihoa miller bird
noisy scrub-bird
Norfolk Island parakeet
orange-bellied parakeet
orange-fronted parakeet
ou
Palau ground dove
Palau megapode
Palau owl
palila
peregrine falcon
piopio
Ponape great white-eye
Ponape Mountain starling
Puerto Rico parrot
Puerto Rico plain pigeon
Puerto Rico whippoorwill
pygmy swift
quetzal
red-billed curassow
red-faced malkoha cuckoo
Reunion cuckoo shrike
Reunion harrier
Reunion olivaceous bulbul
Reunion petrel

St. Lucia parrot
St. Lucia wren
St. Vincent parrot
St. Vincent thrush
Seychelles fody
Seychelles kestrel
Seychelles magpie robin
Seychelles Vasa parrot
short-tailed albatross
small-billed false sunbird
Soumagne's owl
Spanish imperial eagle
splendid parakeet
stitchbird
Swinhoe's pheasant
Takahe
thick-billed parrot
Titicaca grebe
tooth-billed pigeon
Tristam's woodpecker
turquoise parrot
western bristle-bird
western tragopan
western whipbird
white-eared pheasant
white-winged wood duck
whooping crane
Zapata rail

Endangered Reptiles

African dwarf crocodile
African slender-snouted crocodile
Aldakia giant tortoise
American alligator
American crocodile
angulated tortoise
Apaporis River caiman
aquatic box turtle
Atlantic leatherback turtle
Atlantic ridley turtle

Australian fresh-water crocodile
Australian salt-water crocodile
Australian tiger snake
Bengal monitor
Berlandier's tortoise
black caiman
black legless lizard
black soft-shell turtle
blunt-nosed leopard lizard
bolson tortoise

broad-snouted caiman
Burmese peacock turtle
Chatham Island tortoise
Chinese alligator
Cuban crocodile
desert monitor
desert tortoise
estuarine crocodile
Fea's chameleon
Galapagos land iguana
Galapagos turtle
gavial
geometric tortoise
giant garter snake
gopher tortoise
ground lizard
Guenther's gecko
hawksbill turtle
Indian flop-shell turtle
Indian python
Indian sawback turtle
Indian soft-shell turtle
Jamaican boa
Jamaican iguana
Jamaican snake
Komodo dragon
leathery turtle
Magdalena spectacled caiman

marsh crocodile
Mexican ridley sea turtle
Morelet's crocodile
Nile crocodile
Orinoco crocodile
Pacific leatherback turtle
peacock soft-shell turtle
Philippine crocodile
Plate Island boa
rayed tortoise
river terrapin
Round Island boa
sailfin lizard
San Francisco garter snake
Serpent Isle gecko
short-necked turtle
Siamese crocodile
snake-waiting skink
South American river turtle
spectacled caiman
spotted pond turtle
Telfair's skink
Terecay turtle
three-keeled Asian turtle
Tomistoma
two-striped garter snake
water box turtle
yellow monitor

Endangered Amphibians

African viviparous toad
black toad
California tiger salamander
Cameroon toad
Chinese giant salamander
garden slender salamander
Georgia blind salamander
Houston toad
Israel painted frog
Japanese giant salamander

Mariposa salamander
Monteverde toad
Ocoee salamander
Panamanian golden frog
pine-barrens tree frog
Plethodontid salamander
San Marcos salamander
Santa Cruz long-toed salamander
Texas blind salamander
Valdina Farms salamander

Books to read

There are many exciting and interesting children's books about endangered animals, conservation, and ecology. You can find them in your school or public library. Here are just a very few.

Ages 5 to 8

The Big Island, by Julian May
1969, Follett
How a herd of moose and a pack of wolves live together in perfect balance on an island far from people.

Birds Will Come to You, by Charles Phillip Fox
1963, Reilly & Lee
A book that tells how to make your yard a favorite place for birds and how to help birds survive in winter. Pictures and diagrams show how to build birdhouses and bird feeders.

Elsa, by Joy Adamson
1963, Pantheon
A picture book of photographs that tell the story of Elsa the lioness. Elsa was raised from a cub by Joy Adamson and her husband and became their friend and pet. Joy Adamson told the full story of Elsa in the book *Born Free.*

The Flight of the Snow Goose, by Berniece Freshet
1970, Crown
The adventures of a family of snow geese. Migrating south they are endangered by a forest fire, threatened by hunters, and trapped in oil-polluted water. Rescued by college students, they make their way safely to a wildlife refuge.

The True Book of Conservation, by Richard Gates
1959, Childrens Press
A colorful book that shows how rabbits, squirrels, birds, and many other animals depend upon plants and upon the earth. Sound conservation ideas are presented for the young reader.

Whooping Crane, by Robert M. McClung
1959, Morrow
A beautifully told, action-filled story of a male whooper, his mate, and young. The book shows how conservationists are trying to save these endangered birds.

Ages 9 to 12

Going to the Zoo with Roger Caras, by Roger Caras
1973, Harcourt Brace
A famous naturalist takes readers on a lively tour through the
Bronx Zoo. This book offers much interesting information
about many kinds of animals and how they are cared for. It
also shows why many animals *should* be in zoos—not just so
people can look at them, but so that they can survive!

**Lost Wild America: The Story of Our Extinct and
Vanishing Wildlife,** by Robert M. McClung
1969, Morrow
A book that tells about the ruthless extermination of
many species, and discusses what is being done to
preserve and protect America's wildlife.

Our Threatened Wildlife: An Ecological Study, by Bill Perry
1970, Coward-McCann
An interesting explanation of ecology—the relationship of
plants and animals to each other and to the earth—and
of mankind's role in the world of nature.

Trumpeter: The Story of a Swan, by Jane and Paul Annixter
1973, Holiday House
The adventures of a trumpeter swan. These birds, the
biggest in North America, very nearly became extinct.

Who Really Killed Cock Robin, by Jean Craighead George
1973, Dutton
An ecology detective story. What was causing the town's
robins to sicken and die? Some of the children intended to
find out!

Wildlife Rescue: Alternative to Extinction, by Ada and Frank Graham
1970, Cowles
An exciting account of how four different people worked to
rescue endangered animals in different parts of the world.

The Wolf, by Dr. Michael Fox
1973, Coward-McCann
In this book, the important role of the wolf in nature
is shown in the adventures of five wolf cubs growing
up in the Arctic.

Conservation groups

These are some of the major organizations that are working to help protect endangered animals. You may wish to write to some of them for further information.

United States

National Audubon Society
950 3rd Avenue
New York, New York   10022

National Wildlife Federation
1412 16th Street NW
Washington, D.C.   20036

North American Wildlife Foundation
709 Wire Building
Washington, D.C.   20005

Elsa Clubs of America
The Elsa Wild Animal Appeal
P.O. Box 4572
North Hollywood, Calif. 91607
(The Elsa Wild Animal Appeal is also active in Canada, Great Britain, and Kenya)

Wilderness Society
729 15th Street
Washington, D.C.   20005

Wildlife Management Institute
709 Wire Building
Washington, D.C.   20005

Wildlife Society
Suite S-176
3900 Wisconsin Avenue
Washington, D.C.   20016

World Wildlife Fund
Suite 619
910 17th Street
Washington, D.C.   20006

Canada

Canadian Wildlife Service
Department of the Environment
Place Vincent Massey
Hull, Quebec

Canadian Nature Federation
46 Elgin Street
Ottawa, Ontario   K1P5K6

United Kingdom

Conservation Society
21 Hanyards Lane
Cuffley
Potters Bar
Hertfordshire, England

Royal Society for the Protection of Birds
The Lodge
Sandy
Bedfordshire, England

Australia

Australian Conservation Foundation
206 Clarendon Street
East Melbourne, Victoria   3002

Wildlife Preservation Society of Australia
12 Olympia Road
Narenburn, NSW   2065

New Zealand

Nature Conservation Council
Lands and Survey Department
Government Buildings
Lambton Quay
Wellington 1

Royal Forest and Bird Protection
    Society of New Zealand, Inc.
Evening Post Building
Willis Street
Wellington 1

New Words

Here are some of the words you have met in this book. Most of them were probably new to you, but many of them are words you'll meet again—so they're good words to know. Most of them are animal names or words of science that may be hard for you to pronounce. Next to each word we show you how to say it: **addax** (AD aks). The part shown in capital letters is said a little more loudly than the rest of the word. Under each word is a sentence that tells what the word means.

abalone (ab uh LOH nee)
The abalone is a sea snail.

addax (AD aks)
The addax is a large, light-colored antelope that lives in the desert.

Adriatic (ayd ree AT ihk)
The Adriatic Sea lies between Italy and Yugoslavia.

ancestor (AN sehs tuhr)
An ancestor is one from whom a living thing is descended.

armadillo (ahr muh DIHL oh)
The armadillo is a mammal that has an armor of small bony plates all over its body and head.

auk (awk)
The auk is a diving bird found in Arctic sea regions.

aye-aye (eye eye)
The aye-aye is a monkeylike mammal that is active at night.

caribou (KAR uh boo)
A caribou is a large deer of northern North America.

chinchilla (chihn CHIHL uh)
The chinchilla is a small, squirrel-sized rodent with soft, gray fur.

condor (KAHN duhr)
The condor is a large vulture with a ruffled neck and bare head.

cormorant (KAWR muhr uhnt)
The cormorant is a large sea bird.

devour (dih VOWR)
To devour is to eat hurriedly and in big gulps.

douc langur (dook lahng GUR)
The douc langur is a monkey marked with many colors.

dugong (DOO gahng)
The dugong is a large, fish-shaped mammal with flipperlike forelimbs and a forked tail.

ecology (ee KAHL uh jee)
Ecology is the science that studies the relationship of living things to each other and to the earth.

egret (EE greht)
The egret is a bird of the heron family, with long, beautiful back feathers.

Ethiopia (ee thee OH pee uh)
Ethiopia is a mountainous country in northeastern Africa.

eucalyptus (yoo kuh LIHP tuhs)
Eucalyptus trees are a family of trees found in Australia.

extinct (ehk STIHNGKT)
Extinct animals are those that are no longer living anywhere on earth.

floe (floh)
An ice floe is a large mass of floating ice.

gaur (gowr)
The gaur is a wild ox with short, thick horns.

hibernate (HY buhr nayt)
To hibernate is to pass the winter in a kind of deep sleep.

hippopotamus (hihp uh PAHT uh muhs)
The hippopotamus is an extremely large-headed, short-legged mammal with very thick skin.

hyena (hy EE nuh)
The hyena is a wolflike, flesh-eating mammal of Africa and Asia.

indri (IHN dree)
The indri is a large monkeylike mammal with bright black and white markings.

kagu (KAH goo)
The kagu is a large, flightless bird.

koala (koh AH luh)
The koala is a tree-dwelling mammal with a pouch for carrying its young.

krill (krihl)
Krill are small, shrimplike animals that are a food source for many sea creatures.

lammergeyer (LAM uhr gy uhr)
The lammergeyer is a large bird that eats the flesh, skin, and bones of dead animals it finds.

lynx (lihngks)
The lynx is a wildcat that has a short tail and rather long legs.

mangabey (MANG guh bay)
The mangabey is a long-tailed, tropical monkey of Africa.

marmoset (MAHR muh zeht)
The marmoset is a small, thick-furred monkey with a long, bushy tail.

marrow (MAR oh)
Marrow is a kind of soft fat that is inside most bones.

Mediterranean (mehd ih tuh RAY nee uhn)
The Mediterranean Sea lies between Europe and Africa.

naturalist (NACH uhr uh lihst)
A naturalist is a person who studies plants and animals.

ocelot (OH suh laht)
The ocelot is a spotted and streaked wildcat.

orang-utan (oh RANG u tan)
The orang-utan is a large ape with long, reddish-brown hair and very long arms.

oryx (AWR ihks)
The oryx is an African antelope with long, nearly straight horns.

osprey (AHS pree)
The osprey is a large, fish-eating hawk.

peregrine (PEHR uh grihn)
The peregrine is a large, powerful falcon.

pesticide (PEHS tuh syd)
A pesticide is a chemical used to kill harmful insects that destroy plants.

pheasant (FEHZ uhnt)
The pheasant is a large bird with long, pointed tail feathers. It nests on the ground and can fly only a short distance.

pollution (puh LOO shuhn)
Pollution is impurity or filth.

pronghorn (PRAWNG hawrn)
   The pronghorn is an antelopelike mammal that has bony horns with a black covering.

quagga (KWAG uh)
   The quagga is an extinct kind of zebra. It had stripes only on the front part of its body.

quetzal (keht SAHL)
   The quetzal is a bird with bright golden-green and scarlet feathers.

refuge (REHF yooj)
   A refuge is a shelter or protection from danger.

reptile (REHP tuhl)
   A reptile is a cold-blooded animal with dry, scaly skin. Snakes, turtles, and lizards are reptiles.

rhinoceros (ry NAHS uhr uhs)
   The rhinoceros is a thick-skinned, grass-eating animal that has one or two horns on its snout.

sanctuary (SANGK chu ehr ee)
   A sanctuary is a shelter for wildlife.

sewage (SOO ihj)
   Sewage is the waste matter carried off in sewers and drains.

talon (TAL uhn)
   A talon is the claw of an animal, especially a bird of prey.

Tasmania (tas MAYN yuh)
   Tasmania is an island state of Australia.

tentacles (TEHN tuh kuhlz)
   Tentacles are long, slender feelers on the head or around the mouth of an animal.

thylacine (THY luh syn)
   The thylacine is a doglike mammal with a pouch like a kangaroo's.

Tibet (tuh BEHT)
   Tibet is a remote part of China.

tiercel (TIHR suhl)
   A tiercel is a male falcon.

tuatara (too uh TAH ruh)
   The tuatara is a lizardlike reptile that lives in New Zealand.

uakari (wah KAHR ee)
   The uakari is a short-tailed monkey that has long, light-colored hair.

vicuña (vih KOON yuh)
   The vicuña is a cud-chewing mammal that has soft, delicate wool. It resembles a llama.

walia ibex (WAHL ee uh EYE behks)
   The walia ibex is a wild goat. The male has very large horns that curve back into a U shape.

wallaby (WAHL uh bee)
   A wallaby is a small kangaroo.

wapiti (WAHP uh tee)
   The wapiti, commonly called an elk, is a large North American deer.

wildebeest (WIHL duh beest)
   The wildebeest is an African antelope.

wisent (WEE zuhnt)
   The wisent is a European bison, similar to the North American bison or buffalo.

wombat (WAHM bat)
   The wombat is a burrowing mammal that has a thick, heavy body and short legs. The female has a pouch.

Illustration Acknowledgments

The publishers of *Childcraft* gratefully acknowledge the courtesy of the following artists, photographers, publishers, agencies, and corporations for illustrations in this volume. When all the illustrations for a sequence of pages are from a single source, the inclusive page numbers are given. In all other instances, the page numbers refer to facing pages, which are considered as a single unit or spread. The words "*(left)*," "*(center)*," "*(top)*," "*(bottom)*," and "*(right)*" indicate position on the spread. All illustrations are the exclusive property of the publishers of *Childcraft* unless names are marked with an asterisk (*).

Cover: Standard binding: *(top to bottom)* James Carmichael (*) ; Walter Auffenberg, New York Zoological Society(*) ; Goetz D. Plage, Bruce Coleman Inc. (*)
Cover: Aristocrat binding: Norman Myers, Bruce Coleman Inc. (*)

2–3: Norman Myers, Bruce Coleman Inc. (*)
8–9: *Childcraft* photo
10–15: Tony Chen
16–17: *Childcraft* photo
18–19: Darrell Wiskur
20–21: *Childcraft* photo
22–23: Darrell Wiskur
24–27: *Childcraft* photo
28–29: Joe Rychetnik, Van Cleve Photography (*)
30–31: Audrey Ross, Bruce Coleman Inc. (*)
32–37: Tony Chen
38–43: Darrell Wiskur
44–45: Jennifer Perrott
46–47: H. K. Bruske, Artstreet (*)
48–49: *(right)* Norman Myers, Bruce Coleman Inc. (*); art: Jennifer Perrott
50–51: Dian Fossey, Bruce Coleman Inc. (*)
52–53: Walter Linsenmaier
54–55: Audrey Ross, Bruce Coleman Inc. (*)
56–57: *(right)* Norman Myers, Bruce Coleman Inc. (*); art: Jennifer Perrott
58–59: Walter Linsenmaier
60–61: Jennifer Perrott
62–63: Walter Linsenmaier
64–65: Jan Wills
66–71: Darrell Wiskur
72–73: Philip Wayre, Natural History Photographic Agency (*)
74–75: *(left)* E. Hanumantha Rao, Tom Stack & Associates (*); art: Jennifer Perrott
76–77: Gilbert Emerson
78–79: Walter Auffenberg, New York Zoological Society (*)
80–81: Jennifer Perrott
82–83: George B. Schaller, Bruce Coleman Inc. (*)
84–85: John Gooders, Ardea Photographics (*)
86–87: Walter Linsenmaier
88–89: Lloyd A. McCarthy, Tom Stack & Associates (*)
90–95: Darrell Wiskur
96–97: George Porter, National Audubon Society (*)
98–99: *(left)* P. Castel, Jacana (*); art: Jennifer Perrott
100–101: Rod Allin, Bruce Coleman Inc. (*)
102–103: Jan Wills
104–105: Jen and Des Bartlett, Bruce Coleman Inc. (*)
106–107: *(right)* Dale Hansen, National Audubon Society (*); art: Jennifer Perrott
108–109: Harry Engels, National Audubon Society (*)
110–111: Jan Wills

112–113: C. Allan Morgan (*)
114–115: Warren Garst, Van Cleve Photography (*)
116–117: *(left)* Warren Garst, Van Cleve Photography (*); art: Jennifer Perrott
118–123: Darrell Wiskur
124–125: Norman Tomalin, Bruce Coleman Inc. (*)
126–127: Jennifer Perrott
128–129: Jane Burton, Bruce Coleman Ltd. (*)
130–131: Walter Linsenmaier
132–133: Norman Tomalin, Bruce Coleman Inc. (*)
134–135: Walter Linsenmaier
136–137: *(left)* Warren Garst, Tom Stack & Associates (*); art: Jennifer Perrott
138–139: Frank R. Sladek, Tom Stack & Associates (*)
140–141: Warren Garst, Tom Stack & Associates (*)
142–143: Walter Linsenmaier
144–149: Jan Wills
150–151: Douglass Baglin, Natural History Photographic Agency (*)
152–153: *(left)* Francisco Erize, Bruce Coleman Ltd. (*); art: Jennifer Perrott
154–155: Walter Linsenmaier
156–157: Francisco Erize, Bruce Coleman Inc. (*)
158–163: Darrell Wiskur
164–165: Juan A. Fernandez, Bruce Coleman Inc. (*)
166–167: Walter Linsenmaier
168–173: Darrell Wiskur
174–175: Larry B. Jennings, National Audubon Society (*)
176–181: Jan Wills
182–183: M. P. Harris, Bruce Coleman Inc.
184–185: Walter Linsenmaier
186–187: Jennifer Perrott
188–189: Allen Power, Bruce Coleman Inc. (*)
190–191: Jennifer Perrott
192–193: Sam C. Pierson, Jr., Rapho Guillumette (*)
194–199: Tony Chen
200–201: Norman Myers, Bruce Coleman Inc. (*)
202–203: *(top)* Robert L. Fleming, Bruce Coleman Inc. (*); *(left)* Harrison Forman (*)
205–206: G. Williamson, Bruce Coleman Inc. (*)
206–207: Carl Iwasaki, Time/Life Books © 1963
208–209: Jennifer Perrott
210–211: Victor Englebert, DeWys, Inc. (*)
212–213: Jennifer Perrott
214–215: Peter Tasker, Miller Services (*)
216–217: *(right)* Lloyd McCarthy, Tom Stack & Associates (*); art: Jennifer Perrott
218–219: *(left)* David Moore, Black Star (*); art: Jennifer Perrott
220–221: *(right)* Jerry Frank, DPI (*); art: Jennifer Perrott
222–223: *(left)* George B. Schaller, Bruce Coleman Inc. (*); art: Jennifer Perrott
224–225: Kenneth W. Fink, Bruce Coleman Inc. (*)
226–231: Joe Rogers
232–233: Sam C. Pierson, Jr., Rapho Guillumette (*)
234–235: *Childcraft* photo by J. R. Eyerman
236–237: *Childcraft* photo
238–243: Tony Chen
244–245: Anthony Saris
246–247: Terrence Spencer, Colorific (*)
248–249: *(top)* Kojo Tanaka, Animals Animals (*); art: Anthony Saris
250–251: *(top)* Caulion Singletary (*); *(bottom)* *Childcraft* photo
252–253: Anthony Saris
254–255: Nathan Zabarsky (*)
256–257: John Craighead (*)
258–261: Sharon Elzuardia
262–263: Thase Daniel, Bruce Coleman Inc. (*)
264–269: Tony Chen
270–271: *(left)* Bettmann Archive (*); *(right)* Thase Daniel, Bruce Coleman Inc. (*)
272–273: *(left)* Bettmann Archive (*); *(right)* Jen & Des Bartlett, Bruce Coleman Inc. (*)
274–275: Bruce Coleman Inc. (*)
276–277: Thase Daniel, Bruce Coleman Inc. (*)
278–279: *(left)* Bettmann Archive (*); *(right)* Bill Angove, Colorific (*)
280–281: Jane Burton, Bruce Coleman Ltd. (*)
282–283: J. C. Stevenson, Animals Animals (*)
284–285: George H. Harrison (*)
286–287: American Association of Zoological Parks and Aquariums (*)

Index

This index is an alphabetical list of the important things covered in both words and pictures in this book. The index shows you what page or pages each thing is on. For example, if you want to find out what the book tells about a particular animal, such as the Bengal tiger, look under **Bengal tiger** or **tiger.** You will find a group of words, called an entry, like this: **Bengal tiger** (mammal), 67-71, *with pictures.* This entry tells you that you can read about Bengal tigers on pages 67-71. The words *with pictures* tell you that there are pictures of Bengal tigers on these pages, too. Sometimes, the book only tells you about a thing and does not show a picture. Then, the words *with picture* will not be in the entry. It will look like this: **African elephant** (mammal), 89. Sometimes, there is *only* a picture of a thing in the book. Then the word *picture* will appear before the page number, like this: **jungle fowl** (bird), *picture,* 223.